Pathways
to *Nonviolent*
Communication

A Tool for Navigating Your Journey

By Jim Manske

PuddleDancer
P R E S S

2240 Encinitas Blvd., Ste. D-911, Encinitas, CA 92024
email@PuddleDancer.com • www.PuddleDancer.com

For additional information:
Center for Nonviolent Communication
Ph: 505-244-4041 • Fax: 505-247-0414 • Email: cnvc@cnvc.org • Website: www.cnvc.org

Pathways to Nonviolent Communication
A Tool for Navigating Your Journey

PuddleDancer Press, Permissions Dept.
2240 Encinitas Blvd., Ste. D-911, Encinitas, CA 92024
Tel: 760-557-0326, Email@PuddleDancer.com
www.NonviolentCommunication.com

Ordering Information
Please contact Independent Publishers Group, Tel: 312-337-0747; Fax: 312-337-5985; Email: frontdesk@ipgbook.com or visit www.IPGbook.com for other contact information and details about ordering online

PuddleDancer Press will be donating the profits of the sale of this book to the Center for Nonviolent Communication. Jim Manske will be donating his royalties for the sale of this book to the Center for Nonviolent Communication.

Author: Jim Manske
Copyeditor: Kyra Freestar, Tandem Editing LLC
Cover and interior design: Shannon Bodie, www.BookWiseDesign.com
Cover source photo: www.istock.com, Thomas Vogel

Manufactured in the United States of America,
1st Printing, September 2021

25 24 23 22 21   1 2 3 4 5

ISBNs: 978-1-934336-40-3 (print), 978-1-934336-41-0 (ebook)

Library of Congress Cataloging-in-Publication Data

Names: Manske, Jim, author.
Title: Pathways to nonviolent communication : a tool for navigating your journey / by Jim Manske.
Description: Encinitas, CA : PuddleDancer Press, [2021] | Includes index.
Identifiers: LCCN 2021015008 (print) | LCCN 2021015007 (ebook) | ISBN 9781934336403 (paperback) | ISBN 9781934336410 (ebook) | ISBN 9781934336410(ebook) | ISBN 9781934336403(paperback)
Subjects: LCSH: Nonviolence. | Interpersonal communication. | Interpersonal conflict.
Classification: LCC HM1281 .M364 2021 (ebook) | LCC HM1281 (print) | DDC 303.6/1--dc23
LC record available at https://lccn.loc.gov/2021015008

With our most sincere gratitude to
Marshall B. Rosenberg, PhD,
the creator of Nonviolent Communication

Endorsements of
Pathways to Nonviolent Communication

"For any approach including Nonviolent Communication there are certain pitfalls to look out for. This book helps us stay clear of those and remember the purpose of communication: connection. Furthermore, this book acknowledges the growth and development that we as human beings take becoming gradually more aware of more perspectives to include in our interconnectedness with others."

—**LIV LARSSON**, NVC trainer, mediator and author of
A Helping hand: Mediation With Nonviolent Communication
and *Anger, Guilt & Shame: Reclaiming Power and Choice*

"*Pathways to Nonviolent Communication* has contributed to filling up a big missing part in NVC by developing a systematic, versatile yet highly adjustable tool for learners and practitioners to do blame-free self-assessment alone and with others."

—**JOSEPH MAN-KIT CHO, PHD**,
Lecturer of Gender Studies Programme,
The Chinese University of Hong Kong

"*Pathways to Nonviolent Communication* offers ways to journey into a self-exploration to mindfully cultivate a consciousness of interdependence and shared power."

—**DR. STEPHANIE BACHMANN MATTEI**,
CNVC Certified Trainer and Assessor

"*Pathway to Nonviolent Communication: A Tool for Navigating Your Journey* provides a practical comprehensive tool that sheds light on the journey from unskilled/unaware through to integrated consciousness. It unpacks the granular details of twenty-eight core competencies of compassionate communication via four distinct levels of development. It is clear, concise, and accessible. I highly recommend this as a valuable resource to all who are inspired to truly connect to self and others."

—**SUSAN CARLTON, MED**, Instructional Designer,
Facilitator, NVC Practitioner, Ottawa, Ontario, Canada

"A gem for beginners and advanced practitioners alike! . . . There are practical examples of the usage of the Matrix in various scenarios, information around the different types of borders between levels of development . . . A comprehensive guide for anyone wanting to integrate NVC into their lives!"

—JULI GOROG, Certified Trainer, Hungary

"Whether you are new to Nonviolent Communication or a seasoned practitioner, this book is full of gems and insights to be harvested through your own lived experience."

—AGA RZEWUSKA-PACA, CNVC Certified Trainer, Poland

"I'm delighted to recommend this book! I love the clarity of the examples, descriptions, and suggestions for using the Matrix with one's self or others. The charts provide structure and order, while options and invitations give choice and flexibility.

"Reminders to be gentle with ourselves convey warmth, compassion, and care.

"*Pathways to Nonviolent Communication* offers support not just for integrating the skills of Nonviolent Communication, but also for experiencing greater self-awareness, self-responsibility, growth, and freedom."

—JEAN MCELHANEY, MA, MS; CNVC-certified Nonviolent
Communication Trainer; Licensed (USA) professional
counselor and clinical social worker; ordained interfaith/
interspiritual minister; certified Dances of Universal
Peace leader, Torbay Auckland New Zealand

"Clarity, insight, and wisdom for enhancing your journey!"

—MARY MACKENZIE, CNVC Certified Trainer,
author of *Peaceful Living* and cofounder of NVC Academy

Contents

Introduction

Welcome! The book you are holding in your hands introduces a tool called the Pathways to Liberation Self-Assessment Matrix. The Matrix was developed to support self-assessment of the skills and consciousness of Nonviolent Communication (NVC). Ultimately, the purpose of this tool and this book is to help you fulfill the purpose of NVC as articulated by its creator, Marshall Rosenberg: To create a quality of connection that inspires compassionate giving and receiving. In short, to make life wonderful!

Kit Miller, the executive director of the M. K. Gandhi Institute for Nonviolence and a longtime practitioner of NVC, once quipped that "Nonviolent Communication is an awareness discipline masquerading as a communication process." Any such discipline is a sort of spiritual undertaking that requires focus, feedback, and persistence to integrate fully into one's life. To live from the integrity of any spiritual path and apply its tenets in everyday life requires radically honest self-reflection. The Matrix offers a road map for the NVC path, to help you get where you want to go during that self-reflective journey.

You may already have experience practicing NVC. You may already be familiar with the Matrix. Perhaps you've been living NVC in your personal work or your work with others for some time.

The Matrix was designed to be of use at any stage or starting point on your path.

The heart of this book is an introduction to the Matrix and its list of skills and levels of development. You will also find here additional information on how to use the Matrix for personal assessment and in other circumstances. While I, Jim Manske, am the author of this book, the Matrix itself and all the source ideas emerged from collaboration with my colleagues Jake Gotwals, Jack Lehman, and Jori Manske. And of course the ultimate source of everything that inspired the Matrix is the work of Marshall Rosenberg and NVC itself.

How it started

For as long as I can remember, I have valued three things: peace, learning, and a freebie. So imagine my delight when I learned in the fall of 2000 that an international peacemaker named Marshall Rosenberg would soon be offering a free workshop for volunteer mediators like me. I'd never heard of the guy, but it was a free peace workshop! A dream come true!

Little did I know when I walked into that room that my life would never be the same.

I'd been on a path of personal growth for decades, and I had already been cultivating a career as peacemaker for seven years, but at that time, I'd never heard of Marshall Rosenberg, Nonviolent Communication, or NVC. Yet in all my previous training experience I could not recall ever meeting a more dynamic, funny, compassionate, and clear trainer. I could immediately see how NVC could radically enhance my mediation and facilitation practice.

After that first workshop with Marshall, my life partner, Jori, and I sought out every possible opportunity to learn and integrate NVC into our mediation practice and our life. We became actively involved in the local NVC community, joining both a practice group and the local team in Albuquerque that organized Marshall's trainings. Soon we started our own practice groups, and more and more, we made NVC the core of our lifestyle.

In 2005, Jori, eager to find new ways to contribute, joined the board of the nonprofit Center for Nonviolent Communication (CNVC) that Marshall had founded. Not long after, she received an opportunity to serve in the role of interim executive director. Saying yes to this offer meant upending our life in Albuquerque and moving to Southern California. For me, it became a fresh start in discovering how to share my experience of NVC, which included starting a local practice group in Los Angeles and my first experiments in offering NVC via remote learning.

I also became deeply engaged with CNVC, organizing International Intensive Trainings, participating in several of these nine-day trainings myself, and co-creating with Marshall and others a new organizational plan for our international organization. The benefit for me was in deepening my connection and involvement with Marshall and other experienced CNVC trainers. These constant opportunities to "live NVC" with other committed people led to a rapid integration of my own skills and consciousness of NVC.

The Matrix emerges

In 2007, Jori and I returned home to Albuquerque—bringing the CNVC office with us! Marshall had also moved to Albuquerque to live with his new bride, Valentina, and we all thought that living and working close by one another would make our work more effective and efficient. Jori's term as interim executive director ended at that time, and we dove back into supporting our local NVC community, which had continued to grow and thrive during our two-year absence. Now there were four certified trainers living in New Mexico—including Jori and me—and many practice groups and social change projects in action and in the works. Soon the requests our team received for support were exceeding our capacity to say a wholehearted "Yes!" We had a wonderful puzzle to solve! And we recognized that we needed the help of other experienced and skilled practitioners.

Our team of four CNVC certified trainers in enchanting New Mexico—Jake Gotwals, Jack Lehman, Jori, and I—decided at that time to create an assessment system independent of the one provided by CNVC. The CNVC assessment system, which we had all gone through and which culminates in official trainer certification, typically takes candidates many years to complete. Since we had more immediate needs, we hoped to create something that was more efficient, yet retained the integrity of CNVC's certification process. We wanted something that would help us and others in our community determine who was ready to anchor a practice group, provide basic training in NVC, offer an NVC-based mediation, or organize an NVC-based social change project. So one day, we four sat down with our friend River Dunavin, who was working on an advanced degree in educational psychology at the time, to figure out how we could create this new assessment system.

Shortly after beginning, however, we all fell into an uncomfortable silence . . .

When we explored the feelings and needs emerging, we discovered that none of us could live in integrity with a system that required a top-down assessment, a system that would judge someone as "ready" or "not ready" for the tasks at hand. In fact, we felt a collective disgust at the idea. We all deeply valued living "power with," while a traditional assessment system such as the one we had imagined would be nothing more than a manifestation of "power over" others.

However, when we connected to the need for shared power, we found that a new idea opened up: What if we came up with a *self-assessment tool*—one that could be used in conjunction with feedback from both community members and more-experienced practitioners? River suggested we use a model he knew from his work in educational research. This model would include four levels of development for each clearly defined NVC skill. We all liked this idea and began to fill in the blanks.

Jake, Jack, Jori, and I then worked together for three years to create a clearly defined list of NVC-based skills, or capabilities, as well as a way to measure development from "unskilled" to "integrated" for each capability. We aimed to name and define the smallest number of skills possible that would still provide a relatively complete description of the capabilities and consciousness of NVC. The goal was to create a tool that would support self-assessment, clarity, and integration of these skills—for anyone. Because we wanted to support clarity of understanding and to make the tool accessible to as many people as possible, we also worked to use the smallest number of words to describe each skill and its development. The result is the Pathways to Liberation Self-Assessment Matrix, which you will explore in Chapter 2 of this book (a full and complete copy of the Matrix is also available in the appendix).

The Matrix was intended to offer a lens for exploring NVC consciousness. In my experience of living and learning with the Matrix for the last ten years, I've discovered that we achieved our goal: This is a tool that continues to satisfy and support me in my integration of these life-enriching skills.

Over the years, Jori and I also designed a guided self-assessment practice using the Matrix, as well as group self-assessment practices and a journaling template. (You'll find these tools in Chapter 4.) With the help of NVC practitioners around the world, we continually discover new ways to use the Matrix in the service of well-being, justice, and peace.

What's in this book

The first chapter of this book describes in greater detail what the Matrix is and how to use it. Next, Chapter 2 presents the complete Matrix of Self-Assessment, skill by skill. The following four chapters explore the Matrix in more detail. Chapter 3 looks at the concepts of *strengths* and *edges* in more depth. In Chapter 4, you'll learn how to create a self-assessment with worksheets. Chapter 4 also discusses how to create a personal practice with the Matrix, as well as ways to use journaling and to make a unique personal Matrix for the specific skills you want to explore. Chapter 5 covers using the Matrix with others, one to one or in a group. Finally, Chapter 6 touches on some common pitfalls and pleasures of working with the Matrix.

Pathways and journeys

We chose to include the metaphor of a pathway in the title of our self-assessment tool (and, eventually, this book) because this perennial image symbolizes humanity's never-ending quest for wholeness and well-being.

However, "Pathways to Liberation Self-Assessment Matrix" is a mouthful! Shortly after beginning to work on it, we all fell into the habit of calling it "the Matrix." Although there was no direct inspiration from the movie of the same title, there is something fun for me about having that in common. The movie seems to try to answer the question "What is real?" whereas our Matrix answers the question "How do I peacefully navigate reality?"

The pathways in our Matrix are inspired by Marshall Rosenberg's "three stages in the way we relate to others." Marshall briefly described the three stages of the developmental journey of NVC consciousness in his book *Nonviolent Communication: A Language of Life*. There he used a powerful metaphor to describe the sense of submission many people experience regarding our (and other people's) emotions. He called the first stage "emotional slavery":

> **We believe ourselves responsible for the feelings of others. We think we must constantly strive to keep everyone happy. If they don't appear happy, we feel responsible and compelled to do something about it. This can easily lead us to see the very people who are closest to us as burdens.**[1]

Because of the way many of us have been educated, most if not all of us likely suffer from this unhealthy shift of responsibility. Two examples of this kind of thinking include "You hurt my feelings" and "I'm sorry I made you angry."

Explaining the second stage of relationship, Marshall said:

> **I refer jokingly to this stage as the *obnoxious stage* because we tend toward obnoxious comments like "That's *your* problem! *I'm* not responsible for your feelings!" when presented with another person's pain.**[2]

However, in the language of NVC, there is also an awakening of **needs consciousness**[3] in this stage. In other words, we get that we have needs. We may not yet have the skill and consciousness to include others' needs as well as our own. In relationships, this could sound something like this: "I need some connection right now! Sit down and we'll clear the air between us!" Someone in this stage of integration might not have thought to pause to consider the *other* person's present needs.

Marshall sums up the final stage of relationship, "emotional liberation," this way:

> At the third stage, *emotional liberation*, we respond to the needs of others out of compassion, never out of fear, guilt, or shame. Our actions are therefore fulfilling to us, as well as to those who receive our efforts. We accept full responsibility for our own intentions and actions, but not for the feelings of others. At this stage, we are aware that we can never meet our own needs at the expense of others. Emotional liberation involves stating clearly what we need in a way that communicates we are equally concerned that the needs of others be fulfilled. NVC is designed to support us in relating at this level.[4]

I hope this book supports you in navigating your own pathway through these stages of relating to yourself and others, using the Matrix as a tool to explore and clarify what happens as you make the journey toward emotional liberation. The next chapter explains how.

1. Marshall Rosenberg, *Nonviolent Communication: A Language of Life*, 3rd Edition (Encinitas, CA: PuddleDancer Press, 2015), 57.
2. Rosenberg, *Nonviolent Communication*, 59.
3. **Needs consciousness** is the name used for one of the NVC skills defined in the Matrix. In this book I have bolded the name of each Matrix skill whenever it is discussed. (For the actual definition, see Chapter 2.)
4. Rosenberg, *Nonviolent Communication*, 60.

Whether you are a longtime practitioner of NVC or have only recently been introduced to its concepts, you might find it helpful to ask yourself these questions before you begin working with the Matrix:

- If there was a way you could assess your own NVC skills and consciousness, how could that make your life more wonderful?

- Would you like to deepen your understanding of your strengths and celebrate them?

- Would you like to understand how to accelerate your growth and integration of NVC?

- Do you wish you could mentor yourself to make NVC more effective, accessible, and fun?

- Would you like to support yourself in your journey to become a successful NVC trainer (certified by CNVC or independent)?

- Would you like to experience more shared power, rather than hierarchical power, in assessing your NVC skills?

- Would you like more skill in self-reflection as well as in understanding your own biases and self-judgment?

- How do you imagine that increasing your self-assessment skills could help you contribute to others and make life more wonderful?

My aim in writing this book, and the aim of my colleagues who co-created the Matrix, is to help answer these questions.

More specifically, my goals are these:

- To encourage you to compassionately reflect on your learning and integration of the skills and consciousness of NVC

- To support your autonomy and help you cultivate your self-responsibility for learning and integration

- To help you develop your skills in **observing, feelings awareness, self-acceptance**, and **discernment**

- To liberate yourself from the compulsion to perform for others' approval or to avoid their disapproval

- To celebrate your strengths as well as encourage your growth and learning

Learning How
the Matrix Works

In this chapter, you'll begin your exploration of the Matrix and how to use it. The chapter discusses some ideas about how we humans learn and integrate new skills, then presents the twenty-eight skills and asks you to go through an initial process of self-reflection.

The twenty-eight skills in the Matrix are arranged to start with more basic, foundational skills and progress to increasing complexity. For example, the first skill, called **presence**, inspires and energizes all of the other skills or capabilities, while the final skill, **supporting holistic systems**, requires one to use all twenty-seven other skills in an interdependent way. We chose this organizational strategy to demonstrate two ideas. First, some skills seem essential. They provide a conceptual and behavioral foundation to build upon. Second, all of the skills support one another interdependently. No skill can stand apart independently.

> *The Matrix begins with foundational skills and progresses toward skills with increasing complexity and interconnectedness.*

Each of the twenty-eight skills will be explained in more detail in Chapter 2.

Entering the Matrix

Overall, the Matrix is designed to clarify a developmental process. After naming and defining each skill, four columns describe how each skill unfolds through a four-stage progression from unskilled to ever-increasing ability and, finally, integration. We call these developmental stages *unskilled, awakening, capable,* and *integrated.*

1. ***Unskilled:*** Each progression begins with not knowing. This is an observation that one currently lacks awareness of a specific skill that others know and can capably perform. Of course, no one can be conscious of what they do not know, so it's impossible to assess oneself as unconsciously incompetent (which is another way to describe unskilled). I myself find that it is often other people in my life who give me feedback that helps me to recognize and awaken a new skill. Or perhaps I discover the existence of the skill in the course of living. In the Matrix, we call this stage *unconscious incompetence* or *unskilled.* (The Matrix itself may reveal skills you hadn't yet thought to cultivate.)

2. ***Awakening:*** Once a skill is understood to exist, one may become aware of not yet knowing how to do it. This is *conscious incompetence,* or *awakening.*

3. ***Capable:*** Once effective training and learning occur, one gains the ability to perform the skill with focus and effort. This is *conscious competence,* or *capable.*

4. *Integrated:* Finally, when a skill becomes embodied and integrated, the skill recedes into the background under most circumstances. One might catch oneself performing such a skill with ease. It could be said that this is a transformation from skill to consciousness, and thus integration. We call this *unconscious competence*, or *integrated*.

Learning new skills

To illustrate the model of the Matrix with a capability you likely have already developed, consider the skill of **tying shoes**. Consider a four-year-old living in a culture that uses shoes with shoelaces to protect feet and make walking easier. Notice these four observations occurring across time:

1. For most of their life, the child had no awareness of a skill called **tying shoes**, defined as "using the laces on shoes to secure them to one's feet." The child is unskilled, or unconsciously incompetent, at this particular skill.

2. Then one day, the child notices that there is such a thing as **tying shoes**, but they do not know how to do it. They have progressed to awakening, or conscious incompetence. "Mommy, can you teach me to tie my shoes?" the child may say. Then they get some training from folks with more experience. "Do this to tie your shoes," says the helper, offering a demonstration, followed by focused support. This likely includes repeated demonstration and lots of practice, including mistakes and feedback.

3. Eventually, this process results in the child becoming consciously competent (or capable) at the skill. The

child says, "If I really try, I can tie my own shoes! Look, Mommy!" Now, with focused effort, the child can tie shoes! As their capability deepens, they can even tie their shoes under the pressure of trying to get ready for school on time, but it takes concentration!

4. With enough practice, the child becomes able to tie their shoes without any help and with minimal effort, even tying their shoes automatically while engaged in a conversation or other activity. Their skill is now integrated—they are unconsciously competent.

In other words, no matter the skill, a Matrix can be made for it. One simply defines a discrete, observable skill and then describes the different stages of integration. Note however that in this process, we are emphatically *not* making an assessment about any person's identity or value. Instead we are describing behavior and capability.

The stages of integration in the Matrix are observations of behavior and capability.

Committing to observation, not judgment

Some may wonder if words like *incompetent* or *unconscious*, as used in the Matrix, point to what Marshall would call *observation* or *observation mixed with evaluation*. This is an important key distinction defined in his book *Nonviolent Communication: A Language of Life*:

> **Observation** refers to that which can be perceived by the five senses—seeing, hearing, smelling, tasting, and touching—and by noticing thoughts, a kind of sixth sense.

Evaluation in this case refers to dualistic moral judgments like right/wrong, good/bad, appropriate/inappropriate, and so forth.

Some words can be used as either an observation (descriptively) or an evaluation. For example, I can use the word *incompetent* to express a moral judgment, like this: "You are a menace to society, a complete incompetent when it comes to driving." Or, I can use the same word to report an observation, like this: "An infant is incompetent to safely pilot an airplane." In the Matrix, we intend to use these terms observationally, without any hint of moral judgment.

The following brief definitions are the ones we decided to use in the Matrix. We intend these definitions to point to observation:

Competent: Currently possessing the capability to behave in a specific way. *I am competent to write a sentence in English.*

Incompetent: Not currently possessing the capability to behave in a specific way. *I am incompetent to write a sentence in Mandarin.*

Conscious: Aware. *I am conscious that the wind is blowing.*

Unconscious: Not aware. *I am unconscious of what my blood pressure is right now.*

We also chose to add alternate descriptions for each level of skill development. These descriptions may be less likely to be interpreted judgmentally:

Unskilled: Not possessing the capability to behave in a specific way. *I am unskilled in playing the mandolin.*

Awakening: Becoming aware that a skill exists that one was previously unaware of. *I am awakening to how to enjoy poetry.*

Capable: Able to perform a skill with effort. *I am capable of writing nonfiction.*

Integrated: Able to perform a skill with little or no effort. *I have integrated the skill of speaking English.*

These examples hopefully begin to give you an idea how to use the Matrix to describe skill development for more complex concepts like **presence** and **empathy**. By understanding the differences among the four stages, and practicing your understanding initially with life skills like cooking or repairing a bicycle, you can get more comfortable with thinking about your skill levels at different things. So let's move on to practice!

Recognizing strengths and edges

The twenty-eight different skills of the Matrix are listed in the Self-Assessment Practice Worksheet presented here. The left-hand column names each skill, without defining it. For your first exercise, feel free to use *your* definition or understanding of the words. I've found that the way I define these skills has changed over the years as I continue my training in NVC, and I believe it's important to honor the life experience that brings you to this moment.

The three columns to the right of the worksheet offer you the opportunity to quickly assess your understanding, strengths, and edges of each skill.

Here's the exercise: Read the name of each skill in the worksheet, and notice how your body responds. If you feel confused, befuddled, hazy, then check the box labeled "I don't know." On your first self-assessment, many of the words and concepts may not be familiar to you, *When exploring the Matrix, notice how your body responds.* and it's likely that most of your checkmarks will be in this column.

If you notice a sense of confidence, openness, self-appreciation, or gratitude when you read the skill, then check the box in the "Strength" column. Check this box even if you think you could be more skillful than you are right now.

If you notice a sense of eagerness, curiosity, wonder, despair, sadness, or longing, check the box in the "Edge" column. This is a skill you'd like to have more of!

Note that, depending on context, a skill could be both an edge *and* a strength. For example, when I am well-fed, rested, and feeling happy, I may enjoy unconscious competence with my skill of **empathy**. On the other hand, I may notice a distinct edge around **empathy** when I'm feeling the stress of receiving a difficult message from a loved one.

When you've completed the worksheet, move on to the next section of the chapter.

PRACTICE SELF-ASSESSMENT WORKSHEET

SKILL	I DON'T KNOW	STRENGTH	EDGE
Presence			
Observing			
Feelings Awareness			
Self-Acceptance			
Taking Ownership of One's Feelings			
Needs Consciousness			
Reconnecting to Self & Recovering From Reactivity			
Request Consciousness & Making Requests			
Mourning			
Empathy			
Dissolving Enemy Images			
Discernment			
Living Interdependently			
Honest Self-Expression			
Facilitating Connection			
Patience			
Responding to Others' Reactivity			
Openness to Feedback			
Beneficial Regret			
Flexibility in Relating			
Transforming Conflict			
Gratitude			
Open-Hearted Flow of Giving & Receiving			
Cultivating Vitality			
Sharing Power			
Transcending Roles			
Awareness of Response-Ability			
Supporting Holistic Systems			

Reflecting on your experience

Now that you've tried out an initial self-assessment with the practice worksheet, take some time to reflect on what you learned. Consider writing about your experience. I've provided a few writing prompts to start with. When you finish, go on to the next section.

SELF-REFLECTION PROMPTS

1. How do you feel, right now? What sensations or emotions do you notice?

   _____

   _____

2. What needs did you satisfy by doing the self-assessment? For example: learning, growth, clarity, acceptance, peace of mind. Feel free to use your own words to describe your needs.

   _____

   _____

   _____

3. Are you mourning any unmet needs? If so, which ones?

   _____

   _____

4. Is there anything else about the exercise you'd like to reflect more deeply on?

   _____

   _____

   _____

Looking ahead

Congratulations! You have begun your journey!

If you chose to do the practice worksheet, you have established a trailhead for your trek along your chosen pathways. After working with the Matrix for a while, you might find that returning to your first practice sheet will help you understand and celebrate your progress.

As you continue to work with the Matrix, you will likely become more aware of each of the skills. You'll become aware of how and when using each skill comes with ease, and when access to a skill seems like an impossible dream. As with learning anything new, consider cultivating gentleness, patience, and an intention to practice.

To support learning, cultivate gentleness, patience, and an intention to practice.

Next, I offer you some choices for which direction to head next on your journey. I love that NVC reminds me of my power to choose! Here are some choices to consider:

- Finish reading the book, chapter by chapter, then return to this page.

- Read through the entire Matrix, presented skill by skill in Chapter 2.

- Read and meditate upon the Matrix. Take as much time as you like to contemplate how the skills live in your experience and what they mean to you.

- Choose one skill you consider a strength, and write in your journal some celebrations of how you've used that strength in your life. (See Chapter 3 for more about strengths and edges. See Chapter 4 for journaling prompts.)

- Choose an edge you would like to work on and follow the instructions in Chapter 4 to begin your practice. (Look to Chapter 3 for more clarification about strengths and edges.)

- Take a walk or find another way to cultivate your vitality!

- Fulfill the request that's emerging from your needs right now!

- Something else!

Appreciating new beginnings

Thinking back on that day when I first encountered Marshall Rosenberg, a wave of gratitude and inspiration washes over me. On that day, I discovered that I had something in common with you and with every single person on the planet, and that I could therefore connect with anyone. I began understanding that universal human needs could become a key to unlocking conflict in my own life and also support my mission of helping others navigate the painful disconnections that cried out for mediation. As I put what I learned into practice, I also learned that NVC consisted of a set of skills that anyone can learn. And that these skills could be our best chance, as a *NVC skills are skills anyone can learn.* society, to undo the harms that have been done to one another and to our planet.

Now, as you contemplate your next steps, I invite you to join me in Marshall's mission to "make life more wonderful" by practicing and integrating the skills and consciousness of NVC.

2

Exploring the Matrix
of Self-Assessment

This chapter focuses on each of the Matrix skills, defines that skill, and describes four levels of development of that specific skill in a sequence that moves from unskilled to awakening to capable to integrated.

Each of the following twenty-eight Skills of the Matrix will have these elements:

NAME OF THE SKILL

A brief definition of the skill.

The developmental sequence from unskilled to integrated through four levels:

UNSKILLED	AWAKENING	CAPABLE	INTEGRATED
No knowledge of the skill	Becoming aware of the skill	Able to use the skill with effort	Naturally uses the skill with ease and flow
Unconsciously incompetent	*Consciously incompetent*	*Consciously competent*	*Unconsciously competent*
A description of behaviors at the unskilled level.	A description of behaviors at the awakening level.	A description of behaviors at the capable level.	A description of behaviors at the integrated level.

The chapters that follow outline a variety of ways you might use the Matrix in your own path to growing your NVC skills and consciousness, whether on your own (Chapters 3 and 4) or with others (Chapter 5). The final chapter of this book offers some perspective on suggested practices for working with the Matrix, based on my years of experience using it, both alone and in company with others, to learn NVC.

PRESENCE

Being attentive to what is happening right now.
Not lost in thinking, emotional reaction, etc.

UNSKILLED	AWAKENING	CAPABLE	INTEGRATED
No knowledge of the skill	Becoming aware of the skill	Able to use the skill with effort	Naturally uses the skill with ease and flow
Unconsciously incompetent	*Consciously incompetent*	*Consciously competent*	*Unconsciously competent*
Unconsciously lost in the past or the future; identified with thinking and doing.	Becoming aware of the difference between being alert to what is actually happening and being lost in thought.	Able to witness thoughts and feelings; able to respond rather than react; able to bring oneself back to alertness when aware of having been lost in thought.	Relaxed alertness to what is happening in each moment, with a deep sense of purpose and choice; openness to what is, with resourcefulness, interdependence, and a perspective of past and future.

OBSERVING

Noticing (and possibly describing) our sensory and mental experiences, and distinguishing these experiences from the interpretations we ascribe to them.

UNSKILLED	AWAKENING	CAPABLE	INTEGRATED
No knowledge of the skill	Becoming aware of the skill	Able to use the skill with effort	Naturally uses the skill with ease and flow
Unconsciously incompetent	*Consciously incompetent*	*Consciously competent*	*Unconsciously competent*
Habitually confuses interpretation with observation; assumes that evaluations and interpretations are facts.	Becoming aware of interpretations as distinct from observations when reviewing past events; little skill or clarity of this distinction when interacting in real time.	Increasingly remembering and making the distinction between observation and interpretation.	Effortlessly able to distinguish observations from interpretations.

FEELINGS AWARENESS

Being able to identify and experience our
physical sensations and emotions.

UNSKILLED	AWAKENING	CAPABLE	INTEGRATED
No knowledge of the skill	Becoming aware of the skill	Able to use the skill with effort	Naturally uses the skill with ease and flow
Unconsciously incompetent	*Consciously incompetent*	*Consciously competent*	*Unconsciously competent*
Little or no understanding of emotions; identifies with and/or resists emotions.	Beginning to notice and have a sense that feelings have value.	Able to recognize, accept, and allow emotional experience with effort.	Effortless recognition, acceptance, and allowing of emotional experience.

SELF-ACCEPTANCE

Accepting oneself with unconditional caring.

UNSKILLED	AWAKENING	CAPABLE	INTEGRATED
No knowledge of the skill	Becoming aware of the skill	Able to use the skill with effort	Naturally uses the skill with ease and flow
Unconsciously incompetent	*Consciously incompetent*	*Consciously competent*	*Unconsciously competent*
Habitual reactive patterns of self-judgment characterized by shame, self-blame, self-criticism, defensiveness, or self-aggrandizement.	Noticing self-judgment, and realizing the costs to one's own well-being; yearning for **self-acceptance.**	Increasing acceptance of, and life-enriching response to, what one feels, thinks, needs, and does.	Being clear and caring with oneself.

TAKING OWNERSHIP OF ONE'S FEELINGS

*Living from the knowledge that I alone cause
my emotions—my emotions are not caused by others.*

UNSKILLED	AWAKENING	CAPABLE	INTEGRATED
No knowledge of the skill	Becoming aware of the skill	Able to use the skill with effort	Naturally uses the skill with ease and flow
Unconsciously incompetent	*Consciously incompetent*	*Consciously competent*	*Unconsciously competent*
When feelings arise, credits or blames self, others, or external circumstances.	Sometimes observes oneself blaming and criticizing; unclear how to take ownership of one's feelings.	Capable of noticing when triggered, and uses that as a signal to self-connect.	Living from the understanding that one's emotional experience emerges from the state of one's own needs and quality of thinking.

NEEDS CONSCIOUSNESS

*Being aware of (and willing to honor) needs—the essential, universal,
elemental qualities of life (like sustenance, love, and meaning).*

UNSKILLED	AWAKENING	CAPABLE	INTEGRATED
No knowledge of the skill	Becoming aware of the skill	Able to use the skill with effort	Naturally uses the skill with ease and flow
Unconsciously incompetent	*Consciously incompetent*	*Consciously competent*	*Unconsciously competent*
Not aware of universal needs; treats strategies like needs, resulting in attachment and resistance.	Intellectual understanding of universal needs; confuses need with strategy, thinking one must have a particular strategy.	Sees difference between needs and strategies; has a vocabulary to express feelings and needs; connects feelings with underlying needs (sometimes with effort, particularly when triggered).	Living from the awareness that everything humans do is an attempt (effective or not) to survive and thrive.

RECONNECTING TO SELF & RECOVERING FROM REACTIVITY[1]

Reactivity is internal resistance to what is.
Recovery is letting go of that resistance. Reconnecting to self is
*being with one's own experience with **presence** and compassion.*

UNSKILLED	AWAKENING	CAPABLE	INTEGRATED
No knowledge of the skill	Becoming aware of the skill	Able to use the skill with effort	Naturally uses the skill with ease and flow
Unconsciously incompetent	*Consciously incompetent*	*Consciously competent*	*Unconsciously competent*
Mostly unconscious of habitual reactive patterns.	Sometimes notices habitual patterns and remembers that **empathy** and/ or honesty were options.	When triggered, generally remembers there is a choice; first response is typically **empathy** and/or honesty.	Notices internal constriction and naturally opens.

1. Some people describe this skill as self-empathy.

REQUEST CONSCIOUSNESS & MAKING REQUESTS

Being willing to ask for what one wants, with openness to any response; not attached to any particular outcome.

UNSKILLED	AWAKENING	CAPABLE	INTEGRATED
No knowledge of the skill	Becoming aware of the skill	Able to use the skill with effort	Naturally uses the skill with ease and flow
Unconsciously incompetent	*Consciously incompetent*	*Consciously competent*	*Unconsciously competent*
Demands what one wants or is unwilling/unable to ask for what one wants.	Becoming aware of how attachment, making demands, and failing to ask for what one wants are less likely to address needs.	Generally willing and able to make specific requests, and when noticing attachment to a specific strategy, strives to move from constriction to openness and creativity.	Willingness to ask for what one wants; has **presence**, creativity, and compassion, even when the response is "no."

MOURNING

Transforming the suffering of loss; letting go of resistance to what is and being willing to allow our experience to unfold.

UNSKILLED	AWAKENING	CAPABLE	INTEGRATED
No knowledge of the skill	Becoming aware of the skill	Able to use the skill with effort	Naturally uses the skill with ease and flow
Unconsciously incompetent	*Consciously incompetent*	*Consciously competent*	*Unconsciously competent*
Blames self, others, or external circumstances for loss; resists feelings of loss; tries to be "strong" or hide feelings from others.	Becoming aware of own tendency toward resistance or blame when experiencing loss.	Noticing avoidance or blame related to loss, one lets go of believing something is wrong and allows oneself to experience one's feelings, opening to a connection to needs.	Fully engaged in the wholeness of life in the **presence** of loss.

EMPATHY

Being present with another's experience,
with unconditional acceptance of the person.

UNSKILLED	AWAKENING	CAPABLE	INTEGRATED
No knowledge of the skill	Becoming aware of the skill	Able to use the skill with effort	Naturally uses the skill with ease and flow
Unconsciously incompetent	*Consciously incompetent*	*Consciously competent*	*Unconsciously competent*
Habitually responds to others with sympathy, advice, criticism, shifting the focus to oneself, etc.	Easily gets lost in the story; sometimes able to guess observations, feelings, needs, and requests (with support of feelings/ needs lists); has dawning intention to give others space, **presence**, and focus.	Capable of being with another without trying to lead them, and able to reflect another's experience without affirming or adding opinions or evaluations.	Naturally focused and energized when being present with another's experience, with unconditional acceptance of the person.

DISSOLVING ENEMY IMAGES

Transcending perceptions that another deserves to be punished or harmed.

UNSKILLED	AWAKENING	CAPABLE	INTEGRATED
No knowledge of the skill	Becoming aware of the skill	Able to use the skill with effort	Naturally uses the skill with ease and flow
Unconsciously incompetent	*Consciously incompetent*	*Consciously competent*	*Unconsciously competent*
"Us versus them" thinking; thinking "they" deserve to be punished or harmed.	Becoming aware of the costs of having enemy images and the possible value of exploring alternatives to punishment.	When noticing one is holding a person or group as an enemy, able to reconnect to the humanness of all involved, dissolving the enemy image.	Holding everyone with compassion, with respect for the well-being of all.

DISCERNMENT

Making life-serving distinctions and choices with clarity, insight, and wisdom; recognizing one has choice.

UNSKILLED	AWAKENING	CAPABLE	INTEGRATED
No knowledge of the skill	Becoming aware of the skill	Able to use the skill with effort	Naturally uses the skill with ease and flow
Unconsciously incompetent	*Consciously incompetent*	*Consciously competent*	*Unconsciously competent*
Opinions and choices are based on judgments of right and wrong; believes one's judgments to be facts.	Becoming aware of another way to make distinctions and choices based on serving universal needs, rather than based on judgments of good or bad, right or wrong.	Has increasing competence in making distinctions and choices with a broad perspective, understanding the deeper meaning and intentions beneath the surface.	Intuitively tunes into one's own clarity, insight, and wisdom to make life-serving distinctions and choices.

LIVING INTERDEPENDENTLY

Living from the knowledge that every individual is related to every other individual—every part of a system affects every other part.

UNSKILLED	AWAKENING	CAPABLE	INTEGRATED
No knowledge of the skill	Becoming aware of the skill	Able to use the skill with effort	Naturally uses the skill with ease and flow
Unconsciously incompetent	*Consciously incompetent*	*Consciously competent*	*Unconsciously competent*
Holds perspectives of independence/ dependence, either/or, and domination/ submission without being aware of alternatives.	Aware of (and interested in) the idea that all needs matter; becoming aware of either/or thinking and of desire to submit/rebel.	Generally considers the needs of others as well as one's own needs.	Consistently open to perspectives and needs of others; experiences others' needs as integrally connected to one's own needs.

HONEST SELF-EXPRESSION

Owning one's experience and having the willingness to express authentically without blame or criticism.

UNSKILLED	AWAKENING	CAPABLE	INTEGRATED
No knowledge of the skill	Becoming aware of the skill	Able to use the skill with effort	Naturally uses the skill with ease and flow
Unconsciously incompetent	*Consciously incompetent*	*Consciously competent*	*Unconsciously competent*
Habitually expresses with complaint, blame, or criticism when upset; shares opinions and beliefs as certainties.	Developing an increasing awareness of how some patterns of thinking and expressing tend to lead to disconnection; starting to explore alternatives.	Usually capable of expressing authentically with an intention to connect, even when stressed.	Expresses with vulnerability, holding everyone's needs as precious; has openness to outcome.

FACILITATING CONNECTION

*Facilitating **empathy** and honesty in dialogue
with an intent to create connection.*

UNSKILLED	AWAKENING	CAPABLE	INTEGRATED
No knowledge of the skill	Becoming aware of the skill	Able to use the skill with effort	Naturally uses the skill with ease and flow
Unconsciously incompetent	*Consciously incompetent*	*Consciously competent*	*Unconsciously competent*
Speaks "at" rather than "with"; debates, convinces, or doesn't speak up for one's own needs.	Noticing life-alienated communication patterns and attempting to have more choice about how to support connection.	Conscious intention to connect; balancing honesty with inviting the expression of others.	Communicates with authenticity and **empathy**; assists people to connect.

PATIENCE

Remaining spaciously present when one feels stress.
An ability to be with one's own reactions, without acting out of them.

UNSKILLED	AWAKENING	CAPABLE	INTEGRATED
No knowledge of the skill	Becoming aware of the skill	Able to use the skill with effort	Naturally uses the skill with ease and flow
Unconsciously incompetent	*Consciously incompetent*	*Consciously competent*	*Unconsciously competent*
Usually relates with an intention to get what one wants and/or with submissiveness.	Impatient or distracted by own impulses; interrupts; tendency to act with reactivity.	Working to expand one's range of acceptance and the ability to pause in self-connection before responding to reactivity.	Naturally self-connects and opens when experiencing constriction or urgency; has willingness to wait.

RESPONDING TO OTHERS' REACTIVITY

*Responding rather than reacting to others who are
caught up in intense separating emotions.*[2]

UNSKILLED	AWAKENING	CAPABLE	INTEGRATED
No knowledge of the skill	Becoming aware of the skill	Able to use the skill with effort	Naturally uses the skill with ease and flow
Unconsciously incompetent	*Consciously incompetent*	*Consciously competent*	*Unconsciously competent*
Reacts habitually with defensiveness, submissiveness, or avoidance when others are triggered.	Increasingly notices one's own habitual reactions and their effect on connection.	Increasing self-connection and ability to choose **empathy** or honesty when in the **presence** of others' reactivity; opening to curiosity about others' perspectives.	Responds to others' reactivity with centeredness; accepts the other at times when the other is triggered; able to be present.

2. I define separating emotions as emotions that make one feel alienated or separate from others. Anger, guilt, and shame are the classic examples. Separating emotions are (for me) distinct from painful feelings like sadness or mourning that do not imply wrongness or moral judgment. I can feel sad without feeling separate. I cannot feel angry without feeling separate.

OPENNESS TO FEEDBACK

Receiving others' perspectives about one's actions
with equanimity and centeredness.

UNSKILLED	AWAKENING	CAPABLE	INTEGRATED
No knowledge of the skill	Becoming aware of the skill	Able to use the skill with effort	Naturally uses the skill with ease and flow
Unconsciously incompetent	*Consciously incompetent*	*Consciously competent*	*Unconsciously competent*
Interprets feedback as criticism or praise, as meaning something is wrong or right with oneself or the other.	Recognizes desire to transform one's own reactivity around receiving feedback.	Understands that feedback from another is that person's perspective and connects it to that person's needs; connects one's reaction to feedback to one's own needs.	Receives feedback as information to be considered, with clarity of choice; aware that others are speaking from their own perspectives.

BENEFICIAL REGRET

*Acknowledging and learning from missed opportunities
to meet needs, without guilt, shame, or self-punishment.*

UNSKILLED	AWAKENING	CAPABLE	INTEGRATED
No knowledge of the skill	Becoming aware of the skill	Able to use the skill with effort	Naturally uses the skill with ease and flow
Unconsciously incompetent	*Consciously incompetent*	*Consciously competent*	*Unconsciously competent*
Takes responsibility for the feelings of others with guilt, shame, or defensiveness; apologizes to protect oneself by assuaging others' feelings.	Newfound awareness that others' feelings are caused by their needs; may want others to "get over it"; heightened awareness of one's habit of self-blame.	Increasing ability to transform guilt into learning, which fosters willingness to seek connection with others (with **empathy** and honesty) when events did not work for them.	Consistent willingness to openly own one's part in outcomes that did not meet needs; willingness to feel and express regret; seeks learning and growth.

FLEXIBILITY IN RELATING

Openness and versatility in interacting with others.

UNSKILLED	AWAKENING	CAPABLE	INTEGRATED
No knowledge of the skill	Becoming aware of the skill	Able to use the skill with effort	Naturally uses the skill with ease and flow
Unconsciously incompetent	*Consciously incompetent*	*Consciously competent*	*Unconsciously competent*
Habitually relates from a perspective of right/wrong, win/lose, "should," "have to," etc.	Increasing ability to distinguish between life-alienated communication patterns and NVC, while reactive communication patterns continue; uses formulaic, self-conscious expressions of NVC honesty and **empathy**; thinks NVC is OFNR (observations, feelings, needs, requests).	Willing and usually able to hear observations, feelings, needs, and requests, no matter how they are communicated; has started experimenting with "street giraffe" to speak in ways that are more likely to connect.	Relates naturally with authenticity and **empathy**; expressions are attuned to the needs and styles of those involved, and may not "sound like NVC language."

TRANSFORMING CONFLICT

Using conflict with others as a means to connect and create a mutual outcome.

UNSKILLED	AWAKENING	CAPABLE	INTEGRATED
No knowledge of the skill	Becoming aware of the skill	Able to use the skill with effort	Naturally uses the skill with ease and flow
Unconsciously incompetent	*Consciously incompetent*	*Consciously competent*	*Unconsciously competent*
Afraid of or addicted to conflict; unconsciously attached to opinions and strategies; takes sides.	Becoming aware of one's own reactive patterns in response to conflict; starting to notice one's attachments (to resolution, to conflict itself, to safety, etc.).	Willing to support all parties in being resourceful and creative, and to include the needs of all concerned, even in the face of one's own habitual reactions to conflict.	Has openness, curiosity, and creativity about different perspectives as an opportunity to expand awareness and take effective action.

GRATITUDE

Finding the value in, appreciating, and enjoying what is.

UNSKILLED	AWAKENING	CAPABLE	INTEGRATED
No knowledge of the skill	Becoming aware of the skill	Able to use the skill with effort	Naturally uses the skill with ease and flow
Unconsciously incompetent	*Consciously incompetent*	*Consciously competent*	*Unconsciously competent*
Focuses on what is missing and complains; uses and looks for validation through praise and reward.	Notices that the strategies of praise, reward, and external validation do not support connection; starting to notice the value in appreciating met needs.	Willing and able to connect to, savor, and express the gift(s) in what is happening.	Lives in appreciation that everything can be a stimulus for enjoyment and/ or growth.

OPEN-HEARTED FLOW OF GIVING & RECEIVING

Transforming scarcity thinking into thriving creatively;
joyfully contributing and receiving.

UNSKILLED	AWAKENING	CAPABLE	INTEGRATED
No knowledge of the skill	Becoming aware of the skill	Able to use the skill with effort	Naturally uses the skill with ease and flow
Unconsciously incompetent	*Consciously incompetent*	*Consciously competent*	*Unconsciously competent*
Resources are hoarded and/or used to control others; one fears loss or not having enough; money and things are equated with security.	Becoming aware of one's fears associated with not having enough, and of the value of contributing.	Increasing awareness of habitual programming, such as desire to hoard or difficulty receiving, and increased joy in the flow of contributing and receiving.	Joy and ease in giving and receiving with creativity and resourcefulness; giving is receiving.

CULTIVATING VITALITY

*Tuning in to oneself to support balanced self-care;
cultivating the energy to serve life.*

UNSKILLED	AWAKENING	CAPABLE	INTEGRATED
No knowledge of the skill	Becoming aware of the skill	Able to use the skill with effort	Naturally uses the skill with ease and flow
Unconsciously incompetent	*Consciously incompetent*	*Consciously competent*	*Unconsciously competent*
Unconscious habitual patterns and/or restless mental activity result in decreased energy.	Becoming aware of own energy levels and what influences them.	Connected to needs as resources; motivated to seek ways to be resourceful and to contribute.	Energized by contributing to body, mind, spirit, and community.

SHARING POWER

Transforming domination; valuing everyone's needs with mutuality and respect; transcending submission and rebellion.

UNSKILLED	AWAKENING	CAPABLE	INTEGRATED
No knowledge of the skill	Becoming aware of the skill	Able to use the skill with effort	Naturally uses the skill with ease and flow
Unconsciously incompetent	*Consciously incompetent*	*Consciously competent*	*Unconsciously competent*
Relationships are based on domination and submission; fears, lusts for, or hoards power.	Becoming aware of domination and submission and of possibilities of relating with mutuality.	Aware of one's own submission or attempts to dominate; strives to act with mutuality and **empathy** for oneself and others.	Acting from a valuing of everyone's needs, and honoring each person's autonomy; transcending domination, submission, and rebellion.

TRANSCENDING ROLES

Being aware that people are not the roles they play; having choice about what roles one adopts and how one responds to the roles others adopt.

UNSKILLED	AWAKENING	CAPABLE	INTEGRATED
No knowledge of the skill *Unconsciously incompetent*	Becoming aware of the skill *Consciously incompetent*	Able to use the skill with effort *Consciously competent*	Naturally uses the skill with ease and flow *Unconsciously competent*
Unconsciously stuck in reactions to roles—one's own and others'.	Becoming aware of the suffering that can occur when people react to roles rather than responding to needs.	Able to respond with self-connection, **empathy**, and honesty, rather than reacting based on the roles being played by oneself and/or others.	Gracefully and easily assumes, responds to, and/or refrains from roles; aware of interdependence beyond roles.

AWARENESS OF RESPONSE-ABILITY

Freely choosing one's responses to what shows up in life.
Owning one's part in what happens, not owning others' parts,
and acknowledging that one's actions do influence others.

UNSKILLED	AWAKENING	CAPABLE	INTEGRATED
No knowledge of the skill	Becoming aware of the skill	Able to use the skill with effort	Naturally uses the skill with ease and flow
Unconsciously incompetent	*Consciously incompetent*	*Consciously competent*	*Unconsciously competent*
Lives in victim consciousness: perceives that one's experience and actions can be caused by others or by external circumstances; lacks clarity about whose part is whose (e.g., I caused yours, you caused mine, or it caused yours and mine).	Becoming aware of victim consciousness and its costs; finding relief and freedom in the awareness of one's power, and still finding oneself stuck in habitual patterns of guilt and blame; diagnoses others as stuck or blaming, and attempts to educate them to protect oneself.	Able to take ownership of one's experience and choices when one becomes aware of blaming, justifying, or minimizing, without trying to take ownership of others' reactions and responses.	Consistently able to respond with equanimity; grounded and centered in authorship of one's own life; clear about others' authorship of their lives.

SUPPORTING HOLISTIC SYSTEMS

*Consciously participating in the creation and evolution
of holistic systems that foster general well-being.*

UNSKILLED	AWAKENING	CAPABLE	INTEGRATED
No knowledge of the skill	Becoming aware of the skill	Able to use the skill with effort	Naturally uses the skill with ease and flow
Unconsciously incompetent	*Consciously incompetent*	*Consciously competent*	*Unconsciously competent*
Rebels against or submits to structures; uses organizational structures to assert one's power, or feels helpless in relationship to organizational rules.	Limited view, overwhelm, and/ or hopelessness about effecting change toward systems that value the needs of those affected.	Aware of potential for systems to be organized around universally valued needs; willingness to contribute to general well-being, with growing creativity.	Engaged in creating and improving systems with the intention of contributing to general well-being, with **openness to feedback**.

The Pathways to Liberation
Self-Assessment Matrix

The appendix to this book contains a full and complete version of the Pathways to Liberation Self-Assessment Matrix. You will also find in the appendix several blank worksheets similar to the one you filled out in Chapter 1, including one that contains the skill definitions we four authors consented to. I encourage you to make copies and return to these worksheets periodically as you progress along your own pathway, and in the following chapters, I will make specific suggestions about how.

As you continue working with the Matrix, remember to pay attention and notice how your body responds when you're considering each skill and how it currently expresses in your life. (This relates to the skill of **feelings awareness**, which of course is a strength for some and an edge for others: Because of the way we humans have been educated and the traumas we may have experienced, we may have more or less difficulty noticing and naming sensations and emotions. Please remember it is always okay to be just as you are right now.)

Strategies for Using
the Matrix Effectively

Since the Matrix was first developed, we've discovered several effective ways of using the tool to support growth, learning, and integration. The following chapters offer ways to use the Matrix with yourself, with a partner, and with groups. In Chapter 4, you'll have the opportunity to fill in your own worksheet for each skill, using the categories of "I don't know," "Strengths," and "Edges" to mark where you are now on your journey. To help you prepare to work successfully with these categories, this chapter will discuss edges in more detail, as well as how edges and strengths complement each other.

Working through edges

As one progresses along a pathway of increasing capability, one naturally encounters borders between levels of development. We have nicknamed these borders *edges*. The Matrix includes three distinct edges: from unskilled to awakening, from awakening to capable, and from capable to integrated.

Edge One: Unskilled to awakening

A person who becomes aware that a previously unknown skill exists is moving from unskilled to awakening in regard to that skill. Confronting this edge may stimulate both resistance to change and curiosity.

Both of these reactions emerge from human biology and become reinforced by beliefs. When we humans settle into a life pattern that seems predictable, our nervous systems naturally relax, and this relaxation saves us energy. We enjoy being able to reliably predict what comes next, so we love it when things stay just so. Change can feel scary, because we don't know what will come after the change. By definition, change gives way to surprise, and some surprises can be harmful.

On top of the biology, most of us have been programmed to beware of the unknown. As children we may have received well-intended messages from caretakers who had positive intentions to protect us. We heard "Watch out!" and "Be careful!" when we got too close to literal edges, like a steep drop-off.

As one progresses along a pathway of increasing capability, one naturally encounters edges.

So, we all have a hard-wired biological program that says, "Stop! Don't cross that border! Stay safe!" And this program is reinforced by beliefs like "I can't" or "I shouldn't." We may have integrated these messages into a belief that moving into the unknown is somehow beyond our capacity to handle or is in some way harmful. We may not trust our capacity to navigate whatever comes next.

And yet we have another impulse. Human beings thrive on novelty and variety—but only if we feel safe and secure. Once we have anchored into a sense of security, we naturally and cautiously venture into new territory, eager for discovery. Sometimes surprise delights!

This is the lesson to remember at the edge between unskilled and awakening: *Do the best you can to ensure that you feel safe to proceed.* From the point of view of **needs consciousness**, this means: Attend to your sustenance, safety, and security, and honor the strategies that help you feel safe. New strategies will naturally evolve as you cross each edge, but only if you feel safe enough to keep on the pathway.

Do the best you can to ensure that you feel safe to proceed.

I remember a time when I was a little boy learning to play baseball. It seemed that no matter how hard I tried, I could not hit the ball. No amount of education from my coach seemed to help. I complained about my lack of skill to the father of the kids next door who loved to play with us, and Mr. Cash offered some simple advice that no coach had ever given me, at least as far as I could remember. This simple adjustment immediately improved my hitting, and I give credit to my adult friend, who had built a relationship with me based on mutual respect and care. With Mr. Cash, I felt safe to try something new.

Edge Two: Awakening to capable

The edge between the skill levels of awakening and capable can also stimulate both resistance to change and an impulse to know and understand more. After all, the same biology and beliefs that affect Edge One are still mostly present, prompting us to value both the safety of the familiar and the novelty of the new. At this second edge, though, some of our beliefs may be loosening up a bit and giving us a taste of freedom from their limitations.

However, painful experiences with feedback during previous learning journeys can leave us with beliefs like "I can never be good enough" or "The teacher/trainer isn't good enough." These beliefs can impede our progress along the pathway of learning. Learning to question their validity can become a powerful aid. One shortcut is looking for counterexamples to your beliefs. For example, if you notice the belief "I'm not good enough," look for evidence of capabilities you hold. All of us have many underappreciated skills, all the result of practice, practice, practice. Of course you are good enough! Good enough, perhaps, to boil an egg, drive a car, play a game, speak a coherent sentence, and more!

Once you are able to raise challenges to your beliefs, notice how these experiences feel. If no experience comes to mind yet, then imagine what it would look, sound, or feel like if you did have one.

Challenge your beliefs.
Seek counterexamples.
Notice how this feels.

You may find the energy of curiosity transforming into wonder.

Curiosity is born of a perception of lack or deficiency. It has the thought form "I don't have something I wish I had—how can I get it?" Transforming to wonder, one tastes abundance, as wonder emerges from awe, joy, and gratitude. A new belief becomes possible: "I can." This belief is reinforced by positive feedback when concentrated effort delivers that which we most want in relation to the skill—connection with ourselves and with others.

Transforming curiosity to wonder can energize us as we connect to the possibility of more needs met at less cost.

Edge Three: Capable to integrated

The edge between capable and integrated tends to generate less resistance. Once we reach the capable skill level, we begin to experience the satisfaction of more needs met at less cost, which generates energy we can use to continue to integrate. We enjoy momentum.

As we cross this edge, we may also notice a heightened awareness of both pain and suffering, as well as increased access to generative emotions like gratitude, joy, inspiration, and love.

One puzzle to work out here can be the *positivity bias*, which is a temporary inability to perceive our edges. Here, we benefit not only from honest self-assessment, but also from feedback from community members and practitioners who enjoy the benefits of deepening integration of the skills we pursue.

The twin energies of despair and gratitude combine to fuel the leap from capable to integrated. This leap is a metaphor for the profound shift in consciousness to integration. Sometimes this leap arises suddenly, like a eureka moment of insight. Other times, the shift is so seamlessly gradual that we may only notice we have made the leap after the fact.

In fact, working with both despair and gratitude acts as an accelerator for integration. On the Matrix, despair relates to the skills of **mourning** and **beneficial regret**, and **gratitude** is a skill on its own. Both types of inner work release energy, and many basic processes of NVC support practitioners in navigating both despair and gratitude. The more I integrate NVC from skills to consciousness, the more I understand that the underlying energy of despair and gratitude is the same. When I live from this understanding, I have more ease in accepting my pain and empathizing with the pain of others.

E. B. White sums it up well when he says, "If the world were merely seductive, that would be easy. If it were merely challenging, that would be no problem. But I arise in the morning torn between a desire to improve (or save) the world and a desire to enjoy (or savor) the world. This makes it hard to plan the day."[1]

Living NVC solves this problem because every moment, whether filled with the pain of despair or the pleasure of gratitude, becomes an opportunity to practice.

The final frontier: Beyond integrated

Clare Graves, a psychologist of the same era as Abraham Maslow and Carl Rogers, in the 1960s, worked hard to create a coherent theory of human development. For me, one powerful takeaway from his work is this: All of us humans will remain on what he called "a never-ending quest," because we have no limits to our integration. No matter how much we learn, grow, and practice, there will always be more pathways ahead of us to explore.

There are no limits to integration. There will always be more pathways to explore.

In my life, this recognition often shows up as a huge celebration, quickly followed by a humbling crash to earth. For example, I will competently transform a conflict with my sweetheart, enjoy the moment, savor the sense of unity—the victory! I will tell myself, "Hey! I'm getting the hang of this NVC stuff!"

And then ten seconds later, or the next hour, or the next day, something emerges from my mouth that lets me know I still have a long way to go!

---

1. Quoted in Israel Shenker, "E. B. White: Notes and Comment by Author," *New York Times*, July 11, 1969, https://archive.nytimes.com/www.nytimes.com/books/97/08/03/lifetimes/white-notes.html.

Using strengths to pass through edges

A strength represents reliable access to a skill or capability that will help one satisfy needs. Every time we satisfy a need, we gain energy. Every time we cross a threshold of development, we add a new strength. Every strength we integrate gives us more power and confidence to cross the next boundary. By taking the time to appreciate our strengths and how they allow us to feed our needs— and thus feel more vitality—we become better equipped to navigate the next surprise on the journey to integration.

So here is a never-ending question that can become a powerful support on the journey: "How can I use my strengths to navigate my edges?"

Using observation to identify strengths and edges

Over the years, I have learned that starting with a clear observation makes exploring the Matrix more effective.

First, identify something that happened that you found challenging.

Second, build a *specific observation* of what happened.

Whether you're doing a self-assessment on your own (see Chapter 4) or facilitating the process for an NVC practice partner or group (see Chapter 5), you'll want to select an event that can be described as if filmed by a video camera. What could be seen or heard? Where? When? Who else was involved? My experience of working with the Matrix has convinced me that starting with a rich, clear observation supports more self-connection, focus, and clarity.

A clear observation makes exploring the Matrix more effective.

For example, you might choose a moment when NVC skills seemed to be tested. For example, "I was talking with my partner about our financial situation last Sunday morning." Include all the observable details of the situation as you start—less specific observations, such as "I was talking with my partner" and no more, tend to lead to a lack of clarity as the exploration unfolds.

The most effective situations for self-assessments are in the middle of the spectrum of intensity: not too easy; not too intense. If a situation is too easy, all one can see are strengths. If the situation is too hard, one finds only edges. It's in that "just right" zone where one can discover both strengths and edges.

Once you have chosen a clear observation, you can refer to it as you explore the skills of the Matrix. For example: "As I recall that conversation about money, and consider the skill of _____, I notice . . ."

Making Your Life More Wonderful With the Matrix

This chapter brings you to the heart of working with the Matrix in a way that fulfills the intention for which we designed it. First, you'll learn to conduct your own self-assessment of the twenty-eight core NVC skills on a worksheet. Next, you'll learn to create a practice that supports deepening and integrating your skills. You'll then find tips for continuing the learning process and for developing questions and prompts to help maintain progress. Finally, you'll take a look at how to create a Matrix of your own, which may include skills outside of the original twenty-eight.

Completing a self-assessment with the Matrix

In Chapter 1, I asked you to fill in a practice worksheet based on your initial gut feelings about each of the different skills. Now that you've had a chance to learn more about the Matrix, our definitions of the skills, and what is meant by the concepts of strengths and edges, you'll take another look at the worksheet.

You'll see that in the sample worksheet (on page 65), I marked **presence** and **observing** as strengths and **self-acceptance** as an edge. As discussed previously, strengths are skills that you can reliably access, while edges remain areas of focus for personal growth and integration. Having identified my response to these skills, I'm now free to use my ability to be present to work on **self-acceptance**. (Note: My experience has shown me that focusing on one edge at a time keeps me in the zone for learning instead of the zone for overwhelm!) As my journey across each edge continues, eventually I will arrive at the skill level we call integrated. *Integrated* means that I can use the skill competently without focusing or effort.

I note that it can be hard to even notice the skills I have already integrated, because they have become more or less automatic. For example, a skill you may have integrated is communicating in your native language: Although you may occasionally be surprised by an unfamiliar word or phrase, most of your language processing happens automatically. Or consider the child learning the skill of **tying shoes**. Once the child integrates that skill, they no longer need to consciously "try" to tie their shoes. They just tie their shoes with unconscious competence whenever the practical need arises! That's what will happen when you fully integrate any of the skills on the Matrix.

In addition, you may sometimes notice having access to a skill "after the fact." For example, after navigating a conflict with a loved one, you might walk away savoring the connection and then realize, "Wow! I empathized with my partner's needs without even trying!"

Strengths are skills you can reliably access. Edges are areas of focus for growth.

SAMPLE SELF-ASSESSMENT WORKSHEET

SKILL	I DON'T KNOW	STRENGTH	EDGE
Presence		✓	
Observing		✓	
Feelings Awareness	✓		
Self-Acceptance			✓

Take a few minutes now to read through the skills in the Quick Self-Assessment Worksheet (see the next page), based on the Matrix. Observe your responses, and practice evaluating your skill level. Remember that it's okay to respond with "I don't know." Eventually, as you continue your study of NVC, you will come to understand all of the concepts contained in the Matrix and will feel more confident about assessing your strengths and edges. (Feel free to make copies of the worksheet so you can do periodic self-assessments or use the sheets with others.)

Creating a practice with the Matrix

This advice from Marshall Rosenberg echoes almost constantly in the background of my awareness: "Practice, practice, practice!" As you learn, understand, and do your best to "live NVC," you will naturally bump up against your edges. You'll discover these edges when, in spite of your intentions, your communications have unintended consequences that can be painful—for yourself and others. Mindfully referring to the Matrix in relation to these moments of stress can help you better understand where you are in the natural progression of growth and learning.

Here's an outline of a process you can follow each time you decide to work with a skill you identify as an edge, using the support of the strengths you already enjoy.

QUICK SELF-ASSESSMENT WORKSHEET

SKILL	I DON'T KNOW	STRENGTH	EDGE
Presence			
Observing			
Feelings Awareness			
Self-Acceptance			
Taking Ownership of One's Feelings			
Needs Consciousness			
Reconnecting to Self & Recovering From Reactivity			
Request Consciousness & Making Requests			
Mourning			
Empathy			
Dissolving Enemy Images			
Discernment			
Living Interdependently			
Honest Self-Expression			
Facilitating Connection			
Patience			
Responding to Others' Reactivity			
Openness to Feedback			
Beneficial Regret			
Flexibility in Relating			
Transforming Conflict			
Gratitude			
Open-Hearted Flow of Giving & Receiving			
Cultivating Vitality			
Sharing Power			
Transcending Roles			
Awareness of Response-Ability			
Supporting Holistic Systems			

Steps for practicing with the Matrix

1. Identify one or more strengths. Strengths are skills that you can reliably access.

2. Identify an edge. Edges are areas of focus for personal growth and integration. Remember, focusing on one edge at a time can help keep you in the zone for learning instead of the zone for overwhelm!

3. Consider this question: "How can I use my present strengths to work on my edge?" As you contemplate this question, needs will likely emerge. Savor the needs! *To savor* means to extend the pleasure and appreciation of something. Imagine what's it like to savor a favorite flavor, and bring this same quality of appreciation to the needs that arise when you ask yourself the question.

4. Through deepening connection to needs, ideas will naturally emerge. Your brain is designed to help you meet needs! When you make a request of yourself, your brain naturally gets busy coming up with strategies to contribute to needs. Capture the ideas that arise, without censoring them. (I find it helpful to write all my ideas down, even the ones that seem whimsical or even unworkable. Sometimes, within the wildest, most ridiculous idea, I discover a seed that, when nurtured, grows into a nutritious practice.)

5. Next, clarify your thoughts, images, and ideas into a clear and specific strategy. Set an intention to practice your new strategy at a specific time each day and for a specific period

of time (for example, two weeks). Consider putting the daily practice in your calendar.

6. Now, make an appointment in your calendar for the end of the practice period (for example, two weeks from now). At that time, assess and measure the strategy by considering: Did it move you closer to integrating your edge? If yes, celebrate and savor that! If no, listen to that "no." Then tweak the strategy toward something that may serve you better.

7. Repeat until you have met your goal of integrating that skill into your life.

Sample practice with the Matrix

This example shows how the steps for practicing with the Matrix might work:

1. My strengths are **presence** and **observing**.

2. My edge is **self-acceptance**.

3. I contemplate the question "How can I use **presence** and **observing** to work on **self-acceptance**?" and needs for self-connection, **empathy**, freedom, and love emerge. I savor these needs . . . where *savoring* means to extend the pleasure of something, to enjoy deeply and mindfully.

4. Savoring these needs, an idea pops up: When **presence** and **observing** alert me to a thought of self-judgment, I can notice the thought, empathize with it, and choose

a different thought that would contribute to more **self-acceptance.**

5. Next, I clarify and specify my practice:

   - Notice a thought of negative self-judgment (using my skills in **presence** and **observing**). For example, "I'm not a very good listener!"
   - Connect to the feelings and needs underlying the judgment (using **presence** and **observing**). For example, "I feel disheartened because I need **patience.**"
   - Consider what thought would more lovingly contribute to those needs. For example: "I accept myself when I feel impatient. I'm learning to become more open and patient."

6. I will practice this strategy once a day upon awakening in the morning for thirty days. I will do this as a written process in my journal, using the moments of negative self-judging to practice.

7. I now put an appointment in my calendar for thirty days from now at 8 a.m. to consider these questions: "How is this practice working? Do I want to tweak or change it?"

Journaling with the Matrix

Journaling with the Matrix is another way to support your skill development and integration. An increasing number of scientific studies demonstrate many benefits from journaling. (If this prompts your curiosity, please check out one of James W. Pennebaker's books, such as *Expressive Writing: Words That Heal* or *Opening Up by Writing It Down*.)

Here are some benefits of journaling:

- Increasing your clarity about your understanding, feelings, and needs
- Practicing **honest self-expression** in a safe way
- Reducing stress and increasing well-being
- Supporting yourself in solving puzzling conflicts
- Increasing **empathy** for yourself and others

Here's a template for journaling with the Matrix. You can follow along or invent your own way to use the Matrix as a journaling prompt!

Steps for journaling with the Matrix

1. Pick one skill, one pathway, to explore.

2. Define the skill for yourself in your own words: What does _____ (the skill) mean to me?

3. What is working for you in your life around _____ _____ ?

4. What are the barriers to experiencing _____ _____ in your life?

5. What is your vision of _____ in your life?

6. What steps are you willing to take to enhance _____ _____ in your life from now on?

Here are a few notes about the steps in the journaling template. For step 1, feel free to explore a skill that is a strength, an edge, or an "I don't know." Over time, journaling about all three will likely help deepen your understanding of all of the stages of integration. Consider picking one skill per writing session. Consider regular writing sessions. Once a day? Once a week? Something else?

For step 2, although the Matrix already provides a definition for each skill, it can be helpful (and integrative) to define the skill in your own words. The way you use words helps to create the world that you experience.

Step 3 begins your journaling practice with a celebration! This helps to acknowledge that we all share these skills as a birthright, even if we had no name for them before. Each skill represents a part of human experience, *Begin your journaling practice with a celebration!* one that is likely shared universally. The inquiry in step 3 also gives you practice making observations, so work on being clear and specific.

Answering the question in step 4 requires and enhances the skill of **feelings awareness**. It requires a quality of self-reflection and honesty that may be challenging or painful. Here, you may reveal things to yourself that you would like to keep private. (Consider the security of your journal, if this is important to you. If it would support your needs for security or safety, or any other need, you can even destroy what you've written once you've finished.) Also take your time! Pause if you need to give yourself self-empathy or call a friend if you need **empathy**.

Step 5 asks you to envision the skill you're focusing on as active in your life. I sometimes call this step "dreaming in NVC." It's likely to awaken **needs consciousness**. It's okay if you experience the images that arise as hazy or unclear. Feel free to experiment with different time frames. For example, what is your vision for living with this skill in three months? Six months? One year? Five years?

What is your vision for living with this skill in three months? Six months? A year?

Finally, step 6 awakens us to make clear and specific requests of ourselves. This can include asking ourselves to make requests of others. You increase the likelihood of getting your needs met the more you make your requests concrete, specific, present, and connected to needs. Remember, requests are like preferences. You can be happy whether or not you get what you ask for!

Making your own Matrix

When my colleagues and I designed the Matrix, we understood that we were making choices about what skills to include and which to exclude. The skill set for practicing NVC likely contains many skills that we did not include.

We wanted our Matrix to offer the smallest number of skills possible to provide a "complete enough" map of the journey to integration. We understood that others would likely discover or prioritize different skills. For instance, I've made a list for myself that includes some of these other skills. At last count, there were about forty additional skills in my list, and yet the original twenty-eight have also served me well without the additions.

It may be different for you! The conditions of your own life experience, your culture, or your predispositions may lead you to create a Matrix for skills we did not even know to include!

So, here's a template for making your own Matrix:

Steps for making your own Matrix

1. Choose a specific skill. Name it and define it.

2. Consider how you or others would behave if you had never heard of the skill. This experience points to a description of unconscious incompetence or unskilled.

3. Consider how you or others would behave if you knew the skill existed, but you didn't know how to do the skill yet. This points to a description of conscious incompetence or awakening.

4. Consider how you or others might behave if you knew how to do this skill, but your doing it required focused effort and concentration. This points to a description of conscious competence or capable.

5. Consider how you or others might behave once the skill became automatic under most circumstances. This points to a description of unconscious competence or integrated.

The more simply and specifically you can define a skill, the easier it will be to make a Matrix.

The more simply and discretely you can define a *system* of skills, the easier it is to build a Matrix of increasing complexity.

Some skills are foundational, while others stand upon that foundation. In the Matrix, **presence** and **observing** are foundational skills required to practice all of the other skills. Simpler skills appear toward the beginning of the Matrix, and the complexity of the skill increases as you move toward the end. **Supporting holistic**

systems, the final skill, requires some mastery of all of the skills that come before it. Our four-year-old, having mastered the skill of **tying shoes**, might enjoy learning more **complex knots**, creating an arc of learning.

As you consider creating a definition for a skill related to NVC, think about where your new skill might fit in the overall scheme of the Matrix. Is it a simple, basic skill, or one that requires foundational skills to support mastery?

Please use the template on the next page to start making your own Matrix.

TEMPLATE FOR MAKING A MATRIX

NAME AND DEFINE THE SKILL			
Describe the behavior of someone with no skill or awareness of the skill	Describe the behavior of someone who has become aware of the skill	Describe the behavior of someone who can behave skillfully with concentrated effort	Describe the behavior of someone who can perform the skill without effort
Unskilled	*Awakening*	*Capable*	*Integrated*
Unconsciously incompetent	*Consciously incompetent*	*Consciously competent*	*Unconsciously competent*
Behavior tends to be reactive emerging from habitual patterns of biology as well as cultural conditioning. One identifies with a lack of skill. "I can't _____."	Emerging awareness of suffering caused by thought and behavior patterns; becoming conscious of signals of pain and pleasure as signals of the state of one's needs; one aspires to have choice in the midst of reactive patterns, desires competence; one has an intellectual understanding of concepts; "I don't know how to _____."	Growing understanding of concepts underlying the skill; practice may be mechanical; one is able to use the skill with effort and increase access to the skill in a variety of circumstances; one has more freedom of choice in how one responds; one has a deepening connection to needs as resources; "I can _____ if I really try."	Natural and unconscious access to the intuitive guidance of needs that motivate action arising from **request consciousness**; one has the intention to contribute to life, well-being, and interdependence; one has an ever-increasing ability to track the development of the skill through the four levels of NVC consciousness; "I can easily and reliably _____."

5

Working as a Guide With Friends and Groups

O ver the years, my partners and I have discovered that the Matrix can be used as a tool to support both one-to-one and group work. This chapter offers some suggestions that we have discovered support connection, learning, and growth in these settings.

Guiding a friend or client with the Matrix

The Matrix provides a powerful template to support self-discovery, deepen **self-acceptance**, and increase self-compassion. You can use it to guide a friend or client on their journey or ask a friend to guide you. Perhaps you'll take turns! The practice outlined here takes between one and two hours to complete.

In this practice, there are two roles:

> *The guide:* Your job is to be an empathic "angel," a warm, loving **presence** for your friend. Mostly, you will listen with an open heart and an open mind.

The explorer: You get to have an adventure! Your guide will lovingly be with you, emanating **presence**, as you explore an event in your life through the lens of the Matrix. This will give you an opportunity for deep self-reflection and self-compassion—an opportunity to discover something new about how to make your life more wonderful.

Note: I usually request that explorers avoid looking at the written Matrix during this practice so they can pay attention instead to their own experience, their own heart, their own body. Sensing the body is the key!

Instructions for the guide

Begin with what we call the Zero Step. This concept points to getting clear on two things that support the process:

First, consider and *clarify your intention.* Why are you guiding this process? What needs are you hoping to contribute to? Do you want to connect?

*Clarify your intention, and cultivate **presence.***

Second, *cultivate **presence.*** Do your best to empty yourself of what you think should happen or what has happened in the past. Be right here, right now.

When you do this, notice that you naturally begin to open to outcome. You become clear on your role as a guide. You point the way, yet follow in the footsteps of the explorer who walks their own unique, emergent pathway.

One possible outcome to keep in mind: The explorer may choose to stop at any point. Please honor that choice, and be guided by them as to what comes next.

Steps for guiding an individual through the Matrix

1. Support the explorer to connect to an observation they want
   to work with. Listen with attention, asking open-ended,
   clarifying questions until you can make a crystal clear image
   of what happened. You can increase the vividness of the
   experience by asking questions that bring the past into the
   present moment. For example, ask: "Where are you? What
   do you see? What do you hear? What else are you aware of?"
   The more vivid the observation, the more powerful the self-
   connection will become for the explorer. See Chapter 3 for
   some hints on making powerful observations.

2. Invite the explorer to embody their felt sense of their
   experience, as if the observation is happening right now.
   Gently coach them to make the experience as vivid and real
   as possible. Ask: "What do you feel in your body? What
   sensations are you noticing? What emotions are arising?"

3. When the explorer feels ready, name the first Matrix skill, then
   read the definition. It might sound something like this: "As you
   connect with what is happening, consider the skill of **presence**.
   Presence means being attentive to what is happening right
   now. Not lost in thinking, emotional reaction, etc."

4. Pause and listen to the explorer's reactions and responses,
   and connect empathically, acknowledging their experience of
   strength or edge. Consider reflecting their observations, feelings,
   and needs out loud. You may also choose to remain silent,
   practicing **presence** much of the time, to cultivate an empathic
   space where the explorer does almost all of the talking.

5. Take notes on what you sense are strengths and edges, based on what the explorer says. Some people enjoy having their session recorded.

6. Periodically, invite the explorer to reconnect with their felt sense of the observation—you might do this after every four or five skills, for example. This seems to support them in staying present to the body. Be gentle!

7. If one of the Matrix skills does not seem to be a fit for the specific observation you are working with, feel free to skip it. Or sometimes explorers will spontaneously think of a different observation that relates to the skill, and you can take a moment to celebrate a strength or mourn an edge before returning to the focused practice.

8. After considering the final skill in the Matrix, encourage the explorer to consider if there are other skills or capabilities they would like to highlight. Sometimes people can name strengths not on the Matrix, for example, focus or a sense of humor.

9. Take a deep breath together, stretch, or otherwise cultivate some vitality. Then, empathically debrief with the explorer. Examples of debriefing questions:

    • What needs of yours have been satisfied by this exploration?

    • What did you learn?

    • What worked?

    • Did anything get in the way of your exploration?

    • Do you have any advice about how to make this process more effective?

10. Summarize the exercise:

- Share what you heard were the explorer's strengths and celebrate with them. This can be a challenge for some, as it may trigger a sense of embarrassment. Many of us learned as children that we should be humble and deflect anything that sounds like praise. Do your best to greet this reaction with **empathy** and understanding, then, if you sense openness, try celebrating again.

- Together, pick one or two edges, no more, and discuss what feelings, needs, and requests come up about these edges.

- Offer to support the explorer in coming up with a practice to work on one of their edges. (See Chapter 4 for tips on creating a practice.)

11. End with some final open-ended questions. For example:

- What are you taking away?

- What else do you need to be heard to bring this process to a close?

- Do you have any feedback for me as your guide?

Facilitating a group with the Matrix

The Matrix also provides groups with an opportunity to enjoy self-assessment. If you offer longer workshops or retreats, consider offering sessions with the Matrix at both the beginning and end of a training. This encourages people to celebrate growth and learning. For longer trainings, feel free to offer a group practice midway as well. The practice outlined here takes between one and two hours to complete.

Steps for guiding a group through the Matrix

1. Provide a Matrix worksheet for each group member. Feel free to make copies of the Quick Self-Assessment Worksheet (found in Chapter 4 and also in the appendix). You can also ask people to use a piece of paper divided into three columns: Have them write "I don't know" at the top of the first column; "Strength" on the second column; and "Edge" on the third.

2. Guide people to clarify an observation for them to use for their self-assessment. (See suggestions for using observations in Chapter 3.)

3. Read through the list of skills in the Matrix, one at a time. After each skill, ask people to check their body, then mark the column that describes their experience. Do this rather quickly to support people in staying in their body experience as much as possible

   - If there is no reaction, or a sense of confusion or lack of clarity, check "I don't know."

   - If there is a feeling of celebration, appreciation, or peace of mind, check "Strength."

   - If there is a feeling such as constriction, anxiety, or concern, check "Edge."

4. Periodically remind people to reconnect to their observation. If anyone asks, name the skill again and reread the definition.

5. When you finish, celebrate all the strengths that people have marked. Ask group members, if they are willing, to share their strengths with each other.

6. Next, invite people to choose *one* edge each.

7. Then ask, "How could you use your strengths to work on your edge?" Share an example from your own experience. (To build the capacity and skill to do this, see the section on creating a practice with the Matrix in Chapter 4.)

8. Divide the group members into smaller groups to support each other in coming up with their own individual practices for their edges. For me, three or four people seems to work best.

9. After everyone returns to the large group, share some tips on how to clarify their practice, when to practice, how to measure the effectiveness of their practice, and so forth. The goal is to support participants in creating a practice that has a form similar to an NVC-based request:

   • Connected to needs

   • Stated in the positive

   • Concrete and specific

   • Open to outcome (and no shame or punishment if someone decides not to practice!)

   • Including an appointment for when and where to complete the first practice, and another appointment for measuring progress after a period of practice

10. End the group with rounds of feedback. For example, ask:

   • What are you taking away?

   • What else do you need to be heard to bring this process to a close?

   • Do you have any feedback for me as your guide?

6

Optimizing Conditions for Working With the Matrix

If you find that the Matrix supports you and those you work with, yay! Use it! If not, yay! Many other strategies can support integration of the skills and consciousness of NVC, and I celebrate them all.

For me, using the Matrix has been a life-changing experience. Co-creating the Matrix with Jori, Jake, and Jack was a profound experience of collaboration. Now, the Matrix supports me in teaching from my own experience. I use it as the backbone for every training I do. Hundreds of participants have told me it works for them too.

I also find that the Matrix changes every time I use it, revealing depths I previously

Exploring the Matrix in a safe, compassionate environment can be a life-changing experience.

had no idea were there. In the process of using it I have discovered potential pitfalls, too, and I would like to make you aware of these pitfalls as well.

We modern humans tend to unconsciously layer whatever domination paradigm we inherited on top of our NVC. Thus, an inner judge haunts us. "I'm not very good at NVC! I should be more empathic! I should be more vulnerable!" My dream is that the Matrix undoes all of that painful self-talk and more! The main point to remember is that the Matrix is a tool that relies on each individual's direct experience. For the Matrix to "work," it requires a safe, compassionate, and empathic environment.

Cultivating awareness

Caveat emptor means "Let the buyer be aware" in Latin. In English we'd say "Warning!" or "Caution!" For me, the word *caveat* stimulates alertness, awareness, and presence, whereas the English words sometimes stimulate fear or anxiety. So what I offer here are some caveats, some advice, some *things to be aware of* as you work with the Matrix.

Be aware of the negativity bias

Comparing oneself to any ideal, including the ideals expressed in the "Integrated" column of the Matrix, can be painful. In fact, any kind of assessment (self-assessment or otherwise) can stimulate a pattern of self-criticism, self-blame, self-punishment, even self-loathing.

Human beings inherit a strong negativity bias from our ancient and vulnerable ancestors, who had to avoid becoming the next meal for a saber-toothed tiger. Even though nowadays we mostly encounter predators in wildlife parks, our nervous systems remain on guard. Our minds restlessly scan for what is wrong, what is lacking, what may threaten us. When we internalize this ancient protective strategy, we wonder in every situation, "What's wrong with me?" This negativity bias illustrates how some of our strategies become tragic methods of addressing needs: With the intent to protect ourselves, we end up harming ourselves with stress and negativity.

The word *edge* was specifically chosen to counteract that bias. Traditionally, strengths are contrasted with weaknesses. In the Matrix work, the contrast between strengths and edges remains important, and frees us from the tyranny of a "what's wrong" orientation.

*The antidote is **self-acceptance**.* That's one reason we put **self-acceptance** so near the top of the list of skills in the Matrix. One's edges around **self-acceptance** can inhibit learning and cause psychological suffering. In fact, **self-acceptance** remains one of the most important pathways on my journey. Like all the pathways, integration of this skill can seem an ever-receding goal depending on the circumstances of my life from moment to moment.

One specific way that I have discovered to work on this edge is to catch myself contributing to life. Here's how: Notice the times each day that you respond with compassion, openness, support, gratitude, and love. When you catch yourself contributing to others or to yourself, slow down and celebrate it. Savor the gift you are giving.

When you catch yourself contributing to others or to yourself, slow down and celebrate.

Be aware of the inner critic

This is a corollary of the previous point. Anything that can become a grading system that implies better/worse, good/bad, right/wrong dualistic thinking can inhibit freedom and rob one of energy. Any sort of assessment practice has the potential to strengthen the inner critic, and strengthening the inner critic can inhibit liberation.

If you get so caught up in doing the Matrix—or any skill within the Matrix—"right," you may forget the underlying purpose of the Matrix, or of NVC. The purpose is to create a quality of connection that inspires compassionate giving and receiving. In Marshall's words, "to make life more wonderful." The stress of comparison and the debilitating effects of shame, guilt, anxiety, and depression can decrease our vitality.

The antidote, again, is **self-acceptance.** Also, it can be helpful to work on edges concerning **reconnecting to self & recovering from reactivity.** When I get clear that at each moment I feel either disconnection or I feel connection, I remember that every moment is an opportunity to practice self-compassion. I remember that recognizing

> *The antidote to self-criticism is self-acceptance.*

my reactive patterns supports my liberation from them. An ancient Buddhist text, *The Tibetan Book of the Dead,* reminds us that "simultaneously with the recognition, liberation will be obtained."

Be aware of any tendency to measure others' progress

I don't imagine anyone wakes up in the morning looking forward to receiving criticism about their deficiencies.

Do you?

I didn't think so.

Please avoid using the Matrix to measure other people and their progress, or lack thereof. (Unless of course you want to ruin that relationship!)

The antidote to this tendency? *Adopt the attitude "I'll work on me, and you work on you . . . but only if you want to!"*

I recall that when I first became interested in following a spiritual path, I enthusiastically attempted to enroll others to join me. I often found myself "selling" my friends some spiritual concept or method, whether or not they were shopping. When I offered my newfound wisdom, I was of course hoping to alleviate another's suffering. Sadly, my efforts had the opposite of the intended effect. Rather than creating a shared experience of emotional liberation, I was unwittingly contributing to an experience of defensiveness and alienation.

Now, I celebrate that **empathy** has more fully awakened in me, and I am learning to offer compassionate **presence** with another in the midst of their pain and suffering.

Be aware of any tendency to make demands of yourself

Please don't turn the Matrix into a new and upgraded system of demands of yourself. You're okay, just as you are, right now.

You can become even more skillful if you choose to.

But any "have to" energy will rob you of power and insight that could fuel your journey. "Have to" blinds us to the beauty we are shining with, right now.

The antidote? *Transform every "have to" into a "choose to"—or a "choose not to"!*

I've had many painful conversations with myself when falling short of my aspirations to show up as the compassionate being I long to be. I've made mistakes, and in spite of my positive intentions, have contributed words or actions that became painful triggers for other beings. But I double the suffering when I tell myself, "I have to be more empathic!" (Or more clear, or quiet, or whatever.)

> *Transform every "have to" into a "choose to"—or a "choose not to"!*

Working on the edge of **awareness of response-ability** has begun to transform my awareness of choice and has increased my compassion for the choices of others.

Be aware of the positivity bias[1]

Most of us see ourselves as having more skills and consciousness than we actually have. In fact, lack of a skill increases the likelihood that one will see oneself as competent. The antidote? *Link self-assessment with compassionate feedback from those who have more access to the skills and consciousness you desire.* It can also be helpful to work on any edges around **openness to feedback**—in any form from anyone at any time. (For me I sense that this will be a lifetime of work.)

Be aware of changing circumstances

One's journey through the pathways of the Matrix will not follow a straight line. Please be gentle with yourself!

Be gentle with yourself!

In my experience, traveling the Matrix reminds me more of navigating an oscillating, four-dimensional spiral than a two-dimensional map, because each moment offers a new opportunity to discover my strengths and edges. I may celebrate one of the skills as capable or integrated one day, and the next day discover previously hidden habits that lead me to wonder, "What happened?"

This is natural and to be expected. Rather than each pathway being a destination, each is its own journey. As Marshall once told me, "Every time I think I understand what NVC is, I learn something new!"

Perhaps the ultimate antidote for any of these potential pitfalls is transforming your edges around **presence**: *Notice your current experience, name it with warmth, and welcome it with compassion.*

Notice your current experience, name it with warmth, and welcome it with compassion.

1. The positivity bias or illusory superiority has been well documented. There are several citations at https://en.wikipedia.org/wiki/Illusory_superiority

The Guest House

This being human is a guest house.
Every morning a new arrival.

A joy, a depression, a meanness,
some momentary awareness comes
as an unexpected visitor.

Welcome and entertain them all!
Even if they're a crowd of sorrows,
who violently sweep your house
empty of its furniture,
still, treat each guest honorably.
He may be clearing you out
for some new delight.

The dark thought, the shame, the malice,
meet them at the door laughing and invite them in.

Be grateful for whatever comes,
because each has been sent
as a guide from beyond.

—Rumi

Translated by Coleman Barks from his book *The Essential Rumi*. [2]
Used with permission and with a deep bow of gratitude.

---

2. Jalal al-Di Rumi, *The Essential Rumi: New Expanded Edition*, translated by
Coleman Barks (New York: HarperCollins, 2004), 109.

Acknowledgments

Jake, Jack, Jori, and I spent uncounted hours compassionately and collaboratively constructing the Pathways to Liberation Self-Assessment Matrix. For me, working on the project in the way we worked on it helped me to see what the world will look like when NVC consciousness becomes actualized.

A deep bow of gratitude for Jake, Jack, and Jori and their contributions to this work.

A final and deepest bow of gratitude to Jori, my life partner. We have traveled these pathways together, and I could not have finished this book without her. No one celebrates my strengths like you do! (And you also do a great job of helping me find my edges!)

Notes from the coauthors

"This self-assessment Matrix is a step toward naming and clarifying many skills that my coauthors and I have found valuable in our own lives. I hope it might inspire you, and serve the evolution of consciousness."

—Jacob Gotwals, PhD

"Pathways to Liberation is about getting free, being free. It was born in collaboration and co-created in a field of cooperation. I am celebrating both the clarity and the connection I have enjoyed during the process. May it lead to the unconditioned!"

—Jack Lehman, MA, CNVC certified trainer

"I love the growth and depth of connection we have had in co-creating this Matrix of self-assessment. Sharing it with others has been fun and enlightening as people realize and celebrate the shifts that have already happened for them, and they become aware of and see how they can develop more capabilities to enrich life."

—Jori Manske, CNVC certified trainer

"I feel eager to co-create innovative ways to help people integrate skills that support them in awakening their consciousness of compassion! This project offers a concrete series of measurable stepping-stones to help you fulfill your personal vision of building a more just, peaceful, and loving world. Working collaboratively with this team continues to be an example of the world I want to live in!"

—Jim Manske, CNVC certified trainer

A note from the author

Since publishing the Matrix as an online resource in 2011, we have been using the version now hosted at radicalcompassion.com/matrix. That document is the basis for all the translations as well.

With the support of Kyra Freestar, the editor of this book, I have edited the Matrix for this project. Our goal was to provide additional clarity and readability in a way that does not affect the underlying meaning of each sentence, and thus protect the care and contribution of translators around the world and provide consistency for readers of this book.

When the four of us finished the Matrix in 2011, we did not have the benefit of a professional editor. A deep bow of gratitude to Kyra Freestar at Tandem Editing LLC for sharing the gift of her expertise with English! I hope you enjoy the additional clarity as much as I do.

Inspiration and gratitude

The consciousness/competence model of the Matrix was inspired by the late Speed Burch. According to CNVC trainer Allan Rohlfs, who knew Speed, Speed was once an employee of the Gordon Training Institute (now Gordon Training International) founded by Thomas Gordon, Marshall Rosenberg's colleague at the University of Wisconsin–Madison.

I'm not sure if Speed was inspired by someone else. When I first learned about the model of Unconscious Incompetence → Unconscious Competence in 1991, from noted Neuro-Linguistic Programming developer Robert Dilts, credit was given to Abraham Maslow. I have never been able to find a record of the model emerging from Maslow.

Martin M. Broadwell offered a similar model of skill development in 1969. (See "Teaching for Learning (XVI)," *The Gospel Guardian*, volume 20, issue no. 41, pages 1–3a, published February 20, 1969, and available at http://www.wordsfitlyspoken.org/gospel_guardian/v20/v20n41p1-3a.html)

Ken Keyes Jr. outlined a similar flow of integration in 1972. (See page 16 of his book *Handbook to Higher Consciousness,* published in 1972, if curious.)

River Dunavin, CNVC certified trainer, suggested that we four authors and co-creators use this form in the Pathways to Liberation Self-Assessment Matrix.

If anyone has additional information on the sources that influenced the Matrix, please let me know!

Of course, the skills in the Matrix emerged from NVC's founder, Marshall B. Rosenberg. Ten thousand gratitudes, Marshall!

Translations

As of the date of this publication, volunteers have translated the Matrix into sixteen languages. I have heard of efforts underway to translate in other languages as well. I am grateful for the efforts of these volunteer translators, whom I guess are driven by their passion to share NVC and make this tool of integration freely available. For me, this is an inspiring example of compassionate giving and receiving! Everyone who has volunteered so far has reported that their work to translate the Matrix deepened their integration of NVC, and that they enjoyed knowing their contribution would serve others. Someday, I hope my wish comes true that the Pathways to Liberation Self-Assessment Matrix can be easily accessed by anyone who wants it in the language they most cherish.

If you would like to translate the Matrix into the language of your choice, please write to nvctrainer@gmail.com and I will support you with the next steps.

A heartfelt bow of gratitude to all who have volunteered to make translations freely available!

Request for feedback

And we rely on your feedback! Maybe we left out something important. If you think we missed a skill, please enhance *your* Matrix by adding to it for yourself. (See Chapter 4 for how to do that.) And if we missed a caveat, please let us know so we can include it in the next update. Finally, if you discover new strategies that you find useful, please share them with us so we can consider including them next time!

Legal gobbledygook

We created the Matrix with an openness to people using it freely and even adapting it as they would like. We understand that the Matrix, or another similar matrix, could help people clarify other skills. However, after working on the Matrix for three years, it was clear among the four of us co-creators that it was "good enough" to publish.

In 2011, we released the Pathways to Liberation Self-Assessment Matrix under a Creative Commons license as a gift to the world, that all would have the freedom to continue this exploration if they choose to.

Please include the following in anything you adapt from our work:

Appendix

The following pages contain blank copies of the Quick Self-Assessment Worksheet, the Pathways to Liberation Self-Assessment Worksheet (with skill definitions), and the full Pathways to Liberation Self-Assessment Matrix. Feel free to make copies to use for yourself and with others over time.

QUICK SELF-ASSESSMENT WORKSHEET

SKILL	I DON'T KNOW	STRENGTH	EDGE
Presence			
Observing			
Feelings Awareness			
Self-Acceptance			
Taking Ownership of One's Feelings			
Needs Consciousness			
Reconnecting to Self & Recovering From Reactivity			
Request Consciousness & Making Requests			
Mourning			
Empathy			
Dissolving Enemy Images			
Discernment			
Living Interdependently			
Honest Self-Expression			
Facilitating Connection			
Patience			
Responding to Others' Reactivity			
Openness to Feedback			
Beneficial Regret			
Flexibility in Relating			
Transforming Conflict			
Gratitude			
Open-Hearted Flow of Giving & Receiving			
Cultivating Vitality			
Sharing Power			
Transcending Roles			
Awareness of Response-Ability			
Supporting Holistic Systems			

THE PATHWAYS TO LIBERATION
SELF-ASSESSMENT WORKSHEET

SKILL	DEFINITION	I DON'T KNOW	STRENGTH	EDGE
Presence	Being attentive to what is happening right now. Not lost in thinking, emotional reaction, etc.			
Observing	Noticing (and possibly describing) our sensory and mental experiences, and distinguishing these experiences from the interpretations we ascribe to them.			
Feelings Awareness	Being able to identify and experience our physical sensations and emotions.			
Self-Acceptance	Accepting oneself with unconditional caring.			
Taking Ownership of One's Feelings	Living from the knowledge that I alone cause my emotions—my emotions are not caused by others.			
Needs Consciousness	Being aware of (and willing to honor) needs— the essential, universal, elemental qualities of life (like sustenance, love, and meaning).			
Reconnecting to Self & Recovering From Reactivity	Reactivity is internal resistance to what is. Recovery is letting go of that resistance. Reconnecting to self is being with one's own experience with **presence** and compassion.			

SKILL	DEFINITION	I DON'T KNOW	STRENGTH	EDGE
Request Consciousness & Making Requests	Being willing to ask for what one wants, with openness to any response; not attached to any particular outcome.			
Mourning	Transforming the suffering of loss; letting go of resistance to what is and being willing to allow our experience to unfold.			
Empathy	Being present with another's experience, with unconditional acceptance of the person.			
Dissolving Enemy Images	Transcending perceptions that another deserves to be punished or harmed.			
Discernment	Making life-serving distinctions and choices with clarity, insight, and wisdom; recognizing one has choice.			
Living Interdependently	Living from the knowledge that every individual is related to every other individual— every part of a system affects every other part.			
Honest Self-Expression	Owning one's experience and having the willingness to express authentically without blame or criticism.			
Facilitating Connection	Facilitating **empathy** and honesty in dialogue with an intent to create connection.			

SKILL	DEFINITION	I DON'T KNOW	STRENGTH	EDGE
Patience	Remaining spaciously present when one feels stress. An ability to be with one's own reactions, without acting out of them.			
Responding to Others' Reactivity	Responding rather than reacting to others who are caught up in intense separating emotions.			
Openness to Feedback	Receiving others' perspectives about one's actions with equanimity and centeredness.			
Beneficial Regret	Acknowledging and learning from missed opportunities to meet needs, without guilt, shame, or self-punishment.			
Flexibility in Relating	Openness and versatility in interacting with others.			
Transforming Conflict	Using conflict with others as a means to connect and create a mutual outcome.			
Gratitude	Finding the value in, appreciating, and enjoying what is.			
Open-Hearted Flow of Giving & Receiving	Transforming scarcity thinking into thriving creatively; joyfully contributing and receiving.			
Cultivating Vitality	Tuning in to oneself to support balanced self-care; cultivating the energy to serve life.			

SKILL	DEFINITION	I DON'T KNOW	STRENGTH	EDGE
Sharing Power	Transforming domination; valuing everyone's needs with mutuality and respect; transcending submission and rebellion.			
Transcending Roles	Being aware that people are not the roles they play; having choice about what roles one adopts and how one responds to the roles others adopt.			
Awareness of Response-Ability	Freely choosing one's responses to what shows up in life. Owning one's part in what happens, not owning others' parts, and acknowledging that one's actions do influence others.			
Supporting Holistic Systems	Consciously participating in the creation and evolution of holistic systems that foster general well-being.			

THE PATHWAYS TO LIBERATION SELF-ASSESSMENT MATRIX

	SKILL LEVEL			
	UNSKILLED	**AWAKENING**	**CAPABLE**	**INTEGRATED**
DEFINITION	No knowledge of the skill	Becoming aware of the skill	Able to use the skill with effort	Naturally uses the skill with ease and flow
	Unconsciously incompetent	*Consciously incompetent*	*Consciously competent*	*Unconsciously competent*
PRESENCE				
Being attentive to what is happening right now. Not lost in thinking, emotional reaction, etc.	Unconsciously lost in the past or the future; identified with thinking and doing.	Becoming aware of the difference between being alert to what is actually happening and being lost in thought.	Able to witness thoughts and feelings; able to respond rather than react; able to bring oneself back to alertness when aware of having been lost in thought.	Relaxed alertness to what is happening in each moment, with a deep sense of purpose and choice; openness to what is, with resourcefulness, interdependence, and a perspective of past and future.
OBSERVING				
Noticing (and possibly describing) our sensory and mental experiences, and distinguishing these experiences from the interpretations we ascribe to them.	Habitually confuses interpretation with observation; assumes that evaluations and interpretations are facts.	Becoming aware of interpretations as distinct from observations when reviewing past events; little skill or clarity of this distinction when interacting in real time.	Increasingly remembering and making the distinction between observation and interpretation.	Effortlessly able to distinguish observations from interpretations.

FEELINGS AWARENESS				
Being able to identify and experience our physical sensations and emotions.	Little or no understanding of emotions; identifies with and/or resists emotions.	Beginning to notice and have a sense that feelings have value.	Able to recognize, accept, and allow emotional experience with effort.	Effortless recognition, acceptance, and allowing of emotional experience.
SELF-ACCEPTANCE				
Accepting oneself with unconditional caring.	Habitual reactive patterns of self-judgment characterized by shame, self-blame, self-criticism, defensiveness, or self-aggrandize-ment.	Noticing self-judgment, and realizing the costs to one's own well-being; yearning for **self-acceptance.**	Increasing acceptance of, and life-enriching response to, what one feels, thinks, needs, and does.	Being clear and caring with oneself.
TAKING OWNERSHIP OF ONE'S FEELINGS				
Living from the knowledge that I alone cause my emotions— my emotions are not caused by others.	When feelings arise, credits or blames oneself, others, or external circumstances.	Sometimes observes one-self blaming and criticizing; unclear how to take ownership of one's feelings.	Capable of noticing when triggered, and uses that as a signal to self-connect.	Living from the understanding that one's emotional experience emerges from the state of one's own needs and quality of thinking.

NEEDS CONSCIOUSNESS				
Being aware of (and willing to honor) needs—the essential, universal, elemental qualities of life (like sustenance, love, and meaning).	Not aware of universal needs; treats strategies like needs, resulting in attachment and resistance.	Intellectual understanding of universal needs; confuses need with strategy, thinking one must have a particular strategy.	Sees difference between needs and strategies; has a vocabulary to express feelings and needs; connects feelings with underlying needs (sometimes with effort, particularly when triggered).	Living from the awareness that everything humans do is an attempt (effective or not) to survive and thrive.
RECONNECTING TO SELF & RECOVERING FROM REACTIVITY				
Reactivity is internal resistance to what is. Recovery is letting go of that resistance. Reconnecting to self is being with one's own experience with **presence** and compassion.	Mostly unconscious of habitual reactive patterns.	Sometimes notices habitual patterns and remembers that **empathy** and/or honesty were options.	When triggered, generally remembers there is a choice; first response is typically **empathy** and/ or honesty.	Notices internal constriction and naturally opens.
REQUEST CONSCIOUSNESS & MAKING REQUESTS				
Being willing to ask for what one wants, with openness to any response; not attached to any particular outcome.	Demands what one wants or is unwilling/ unable to ask for what one wants.	Becoming aware of how attachment, making demands, and failing to ask for what one wants are less likely to address needs.	Generally willing and able to make specific requests, and when noticing attachment to a specific strategy, strives to move from constriction to openness and creativity.	Willingness to ask for what one wants; has **presence**, creativity, and compassion, even when the response is "no."

MOURNING				
Transforming the suffering of loss; letting go of resistance to what is and being willing to allow our experience to unfold.	Blames self, others, or external circumstances for loss; resists feelings of loss; tries to be "strong" or hide feelings from others.	Becoming aware of own tendency toward resistance or blame when experiencing loss.	Noticing avoidance or blame related to loss, one lets go of believing something is wrong and allows oneself to experience one's feelings, opening to a connection to needs.	Fully engaged in the wholeness of life in the **presence** of loss.
EMPATHY				
Being present with another's experience, with unconditional acceptance of the person.	Habitually responds to others with sympathy, advice, criticism, shifting the focus to oneself, etc.	Easily gets lost in the story; sometimes able to guess observations, feelings, needs, and requests (with support of feelings/ needs lists); has dawning intention to give others space, **presence**, and focus.	Capable of being with another without trying to lead them, and able to reflect another's experience without affirming or adding opinions or evaluations.	Naturally focused and energized when being present with another's experience, with unconditional acceptance of the person.
DISSOLVING ENEMY IMAGES				
Transcending one's perceptions that another deserves to be punished or harmed.	"Us versus them" thinking; thinking "they" deserve to be punished or harmed.	Becoming aware of the costs of having enemy images and the possible value of exploring alternatives to punishment.	When noticing one is holding a person or group as an enemy, able to reconnect to the humanness of all involved, dissolving the enemy image.	Holding everyone with compassion, with respect for the well-being of all.

DISCERNMENT				
Making life-serving distinctions and choices with clarity, insight, and wisdom; recognizing one has choice.	Opinions and choices are based on judgments of right and wrong; believes one's judgments to be facts.	Becoming aware of another way to make distinctions and choices based on serving universal needs, rather than based on judgments of good or bad, right or wrong.	Has increasing competence in making distinctions and choices with a broad perspective, understanding the deeper meaning and intentions beneath the surface.	Intuitively tunes into one's own clarity, insight, and wisdom to make life-serving distinctions and choices.
LIVING INTERDEPENDENTLY				
Living from the knowledge that every individual is related to every other individual— every part of a system affects every other part.	Holds perspectives of independence/dependence, either/or, and domination/submission without being aware of alternatives.	Aware of (and interested in) the idea that all needs matter; becoming aware of either/or thinking and of desire to submit/rebel.	Generally considers the needs of others as well as one's own needs.	Consistently open to perspectives and needs of others; experiences others' needs as integrally connected to one's own needs.
HONEST SELF-EXPRESSION				
Owning one's experience and having the willingness to express authentically without blame or criticism.	Habitually expresses with complaint, blame, or criticism when upset; shares opinions and beliefs as certainties.	Developing an increasing awareness of how some patterns of thinking and expressing tend to lead to disconnection; starting to explore alternatives.	Usually capable of expressing authentically with an intention to connect, even when stressed.	Expresses with vulnerability, holding everyone's needs as precious; has openness to outcome.

FACILITATING CONNECTION				
Facilitating **empathy** and honesty in dialogue with an intent to create connection.	Speaks "at" rather than "with"; debates, convinces, or doesn't speak up for one's own needs.	Noticing life-alienated communication patterns and attempting to have more choice about how to support connection.	Conscious intention to connect; balancing honesty with inviting the expression of others.	Communicates with authenticity and **empathy**; assists people to connect.
PATIENCE				
Remaining spaciously present when one feels stress. An ability to be with one's own reactions, without acting out of them.	Usually relates with an intention to get what one wants and/or with submissiveness.	Impatient or distracted by own impulses; interrupts; tendency to act with reactivity.	Working to expand one's range of acceptance and the ability to pause in self-connection before responding to reactivity.	Naturally self-connects and opens when experiencing constriction or urgency; has willingness to wait.
RESPONDING TO OTHERS' REACTIVITY				
Responding rather than reacting to others who are caught up in intense separating emotions.	Reacts habitually with defensiveness, submissiveness, or avoidance when others are triggered.	Increasingly notices one's own habitual reactions and their effect on connection.	Increasing self-connection and ability to choose **empathy** or honesty when in the **presence** of others' reactivity; opening to curiosity about others' perspectives.	Responds to others' reactivity with centeredness; accepts the other at times when the other is triggered; able to be present.

OPENNESS TO FEEDBACK				
Receiving others' perspectives about one's actions with equanimity and centeredness.	Interprets feedback as criticism or praise, as meaning something is wrong or right with oneself or the other.	Recognizes desire to transform one's own reactivity around receiving feedback.	Understands that feedback from another is that person's perspective and connects it to that person's needs; connects one's reaction to feedback to one's own needs.	Receives feedback as information to be considered, with clarity of choice; aware that others are speaking from their own perspectives.
BENEFICIAL REGRET				
Acknowledging and learning from missed opportunities to meet needs, without guilt, shame, or self-punishment.	Takes responsibility for the feelings of others with guilt, shame, or defensiveness; apologizes to protect oneself by assuaging others' feelings.	Newfound awareness that others' feelings are caused by their needs; may want others to "get over it"; heightened awareness of one's habit of self-blame.	Increasing ability to transform guilt into learning, which fosters willingness to seek connection with others (with **empathy** and honesty) when events did not work for them.	Consistent willingness to openly own one's part in outcomes that did not meet needs; willingness to feel and express regret; seeks learning and growth.

FLEXIBILITY IN RELATING				
Openness and versatility in interacting with others.	Habitually relates from a perspective of right/ wrong, win/ lose, "should," "have to," etc.	Increasing ability to distinguish between life-alienated communication patterns and NVC, while reactive communica- tion patterns continue; uses formulaic, self-conscious expressions of NVC honesty and **empathy**; thinks NVC is OFNR (observations, feelings, needs, requests).	Willing and usually able to hear observa- tions, feelings, needs, and requests, no matter how they are com- municated; has started experimenting with "street giraffe" to speak in ways that are more likely to connect.	Relates naturally with authenticity and **empathy**; expressions are attuned to the needs and styles of those involved, and may not "sound like NVC language."
TRANSFORMING CONFLICT				
Using conflict with others as a means to connect and create a mutual outcome.	Afraid of or addicted to conflict; unconsciously attached to opinions and strategies; takes sides.	Becoming aware of one's own reactive patterns in response to conflict; starting to notice one's attachments (to resolution, to conflict itself, to safety, etc.).	Willing to support all par- ties in being resourceful and creative, and to include the needs of all concerned, even in the face of one's own habitual reactions to conflict.	Has openness, curiosity, and creativity about different perspectives as an opportu- nity to expand awareness and take effective action.

GRATITUDE				
Finding the value in, appreciating, and enjoying what is.	Focuses on what is missing and complains; uses and looks for validation through praise and reward.	Notices that the strategies of praise, reward, and external validation do not support connection; starting to notice the value in appreciating met needs.	Willing and able to connect to, savor, and express the gift(s) in what is happening.	Lives in appreciation that everything can be a stimulus for enjoyment and/or growth.

OPEN-HEARTED FLOW OF GIVING & RECEIVING				
Transforming scarcity thinking into thriving creatively; joyfully contributing and receiving.	Resources are hoarded and/or used to control others; one fears loss or not having enough; money and things are equated with security.	Becoming aware of one's fears associated with not having enough, and of the value of contributing.	Increasing awareness of habitual programming, such as desire to hoard or difficulty receiving, and increased joy in the flow of contributing and receiving.	Joy and ease in giving and receiving with creativity and resourcefulness; giving is receiving.

CULTIVATING VITALITY				
Tuning in to oneself to support balanced self-care; cultivating the energy to serve life.	Unconscious habitual patterns and/or restless mental activity result in decreased energy.	Becoming aware of own energy levels and what influences them.	Connected to needs as resources; motivated to seek ways to be resourceful and to contribute.	Energized by contributing to body, mind, spirit, and community.

SHARING POWER				
Transforming domination; valuing everyone's needs with mutuality and respect; transcending submission and rebellion.	Relationships are based on domination and submission; fears, lusts for, or hoards power.	Becoming aware of domination and submission, and of possibilities of relating with mutuality.	Aware of one's own submission or attempts to dominate; strives to act with mutuality and **empathy** for oneself and others.	Acting from a valuing of everyone's needs, and honoring each person's autonomy; transcending domination, submission, and rebellion.
TRANSCENDING ROLES				
Being aware that people are not the roles they play; having choice about what roles one adopts and how one responds to the roles others adopt.	Unconsciously stuck in reactions to roles—one's own and others'.	Becoming aware of the suffering that can occur when people react to roles rather than responding to needs.	Able to respond with self-connection, **empathy**, and honesty, rather than reacting based on the roles being played by oneself and/or others.	Gracefully and easily assumes, responds to, and/or refrains from roles; aware of interdependence beyond roles.

AWARENESS OF RESPONSE-ABILITY				
Freely choosing one's responses to what shows up in life. Owning one's part in what happens, not owning others' parts, and acknowledging that one's actions do influence others.	Lives in victim consciousness: perceives that one's experience and actions can be caused by others or by external circumstances; lacks clarity about whose part is whose (e.g., I caused yours, you caused mine, or it caused yours and mine).	Becoming aware of victim consciousness and its costs; finding relief and freedom in the awareness of one's power, and still finding oneself stuck in habitual patterns of guilt and blame; diagnoses others as stuck or blaming, and attempts to educate them to protect oneself.	Able to take ownership of one's experience and choices when one becomes aware of blaming, justifying, or minimizing, without trying to take ownership of others' reactions and responses.	Consistently able to respond with equanimity; grounded and centered in authorship of one's own life; clear about others' authorship of their lives.

SUPPORTING HOLISTIC SYSTEMS				
Consciously participating in the creation and evolution of holistic systems that foster general well-being.	Rebels against or submits to structures; uses organizational structures to assert one's power, or feels helpless in relationship to organizational rules.	Limited view, overwhelm, and/or hopelessness about effecting change toward systems that value the needs of those affected.	Aware of potential for systems to be organized around universally valued needs; willingness to contribute to general well-being, with growing creativity.	Engaged in creating and improving systems with the intention of contributing to general well-being, with **openness to feedback**.

Index

Note: The twenty-eight skills for the Pathways to Self-Assessment Matrix are listed as bold in this index.

The Four-Part Nonviolent Communication Process

Clearly expressing how **I am** without blaming or criticizing	Empathically receiving how **you are** without hearing blame or criticism

OBSERVATIONS

1. What I observe *(see, hear, remember, imagine, free from my evaluations)* that does or does not contribute to my well-being:

   "When I (see, hear) . . . "

1. What you observe *(see, hear, remember, imagine, free from your evaluations)* that does or does not contribute to your well-being:

   "When you see/hear . . . "

   (Sometimes unspoken when offering empathy)

FEELINGS

2. How I feel *(emotion or sensation rather than thought)* in relation to what I observe:

   "I feel . . . "

2. How you feel *(emotion or sensation rather than thought)* in relation to what you observe:

   "You feel . . ."

NEEDS

3. What I need or value *(rather than a preference, or a specific action)* that causes my feelings:

   " . . . because I need/value . . . "

3. What you need or value *(rather than a preference, or a specific action)* that causes your feelings:

   " . . . because you need/value . . ."

Clearly requesting that which would enrich **my** life without demanding	Empathically receiving that which would enrich **your** life without hearing any demand

REQUESTS

4. The concrete actions I would like taken:

   "Would you be willing to . . . ?"

4. The concrete actions you would like taken:

   "Would you like . . . ?"

   (Sometimes unspoken when offering empathy)

Feelings when needs are fulfilled

- Amazed
- Comfortable
- Confident
- Eager
- Energetic
- Fulfilled
- Glad
- Hopeful
- Inspired
- Intrigued
- Joyous
- Moved
- Optimistic
- Proud
- Relieved
- Stimulated
- Surprised
- Thankful
- Touched
- Trustful

Feelings when needs are not fulfilled

- Angry
- Annoyed
- Concerned
- Confused
- Disappointed
- Discouraged
- Distressed
- Embarrassed
- Frustrated
- Helpless
- Hopeless
- Impatient
- Irritated
- Lonely
- Nervous
- Overwhelmed
- Puzzled
- Reluctant
- Sad
- Uncomfortable

 Some Basic Needs We All Have

Autonomy

- Choosing dreams/goals/values
- Choosing plans for fulfilling one's dreams, goals, values

Celebration

- Celebrating the creation of life and dreams fulfilled
- Celebrating losses: loved ones, dreams, etc. (mourning)

Integrity

- Authenticity • Creativity
- Meaning • Self-worth

Interdependence

- Acceptance • Appreciation
- Closeness • Community
- Consideration
- Contribution to the enrichment of life
- Emotional Safety • Empathy

Physical Nurturance

- Air • Food
- Movement, exercise
- Protection from life-threatening forms of life: viruses, bacteria, insects, predatory animals
- Rest • Sexual Expression
- Shelter • Touch • Water

Play

- Fun • Laughter

Spiritual Communion

- Beauty • Harmony
- Inspiration • Order • Peace

- Honesty (the empowering honesty that enables us to learn from our limitations)
- Love • Reassurance
- Respect • Support
- Trust • Understanding

Nonviolent Communication Research

You can find an up-to-date list of journal articles, dissertations, theses, project reports, and independent studies exploring various facets of Nonviolent Communication at: www.nonviolentcommunication.com/learn-nonviolent-communication/research-on-nvc/

Some of these are qualitative, some quantitative, and some are mixed methods. Together they begin to offer an evidence base. If you have completed NVC research and would like to add your paper to the list, please contact us at: www.nonviolentcommunication.com/feedback-form/

About Nonviolent Communication

Nonviolent Communication has flourished for more than four decades across sixty countries selling more than 5,000,000 books in over thirty-five languages for one simple reason: it works.

Nonviolent Communication is changing lives every day. NVC provides an easy-to-grasp, effective method to get to the root of violence and pain peacefully. By examining the unmet needs behind what we do and say, NVC helps reduce hostility, heal pain, and strengthen professional and personal relationships. NVC is being taught in corporations, classrooms, prisons, and mediation centers worldwide. And it is affecting cultural shifts as institutions, corporations, and governments integrate NVC consciousness into their organizational structures and their approach to leadership.

Most of us want the skills to improve the quality of our relationships, to deepen our sense of personal empowerment, or simply to help us communicate more effectively. Unfortunately, most of us are educated from birth to compete, judge, demand, and diagnose; to think and communicate in terms of what is "right" and "wrong" with people. At best, the habitual ways we think and speak hinder communication and create misunderstanding or frustration. And still worse, they can cause anger and pain, and may lead to violence. Without wanting to, even people with the best of intentions generate needless conflict.

NVC helps us reach beneath the surface and discover what is alive and vital within us, and how all of our actions are based on human needs that we are seeking to meet. We learn to develop a vocabulary of feelings and needs that helps us more clearly express what is going on in us at any given moment. When we understand and acknowledge our needs, we develop a shared foundation for much more satisfying relationships. Join the thousands of people worldwide who have improved their relationships and their lives with this simple yet revolutionary process.

About PuddleDancer Press

Visit the PDP website at www.NonviolentCommunication.com. We have a resource-rich and ever-growing website that currently addresses 35+ topics related to NVC through articles, online resources, handouts, Marshall Rosenberg quotes, and so much more. Please come visit us.

- **NVC Quick Connect e-Newsletter**—Sign up online to receive our monthly e-Newsletter, filled with expert articles on timely and relevant topics, links to NVC in the news, inspirational and fun quotes and songs, announcements of trainings and other NVC events, and exclusive specials on NVC learning materials.

- **Shop NVC**—Purchase our NVC titles safely, affordably, and conveniently online. Find everyday discounts on individual titles, multiple copies, and book packages. Learn more about our authors and read endorsements of NVC from world-renowned communication experts and peacemakers.

- **About NVC**—Learn more about the unique life-changing communication and conflict resolution skills of NVC (also known as Compassionate Communication, Collaborative Communication, Respectful Communication, Mindful Communication, Peaceful Communication, or Effective Communication). Find an overview of the NVC process, key facts about NVC, and more.

- **About Marshall Rosenberg**—Read about the world-renowned peacemaker, educator, best-selling author, and founder of the Center for Nonviolent Communication, including press materials, a biography, and more.

For more information, please contact PuddleDancer Press at:

2240 Encinitas Blvd., Ste. D-911 • Encinitas, CA 92024
Phone: 760-557-0326 • Email: email@puddledancer.com
www.NonviolentCommunication.com

The Center for Nonviolent Communication (CNVC) is an international nonprofit peacemaking organization whose vision is a world where everyone's needs are met peacefully. CNVC is devoted to supporting the spread of Nonviolent Communication (NVC) around the world.

Founded in 1984 by Dr. Marshall B. Rosenberg, CNVC has been contributing to a vast social transformation in thinking, speaking and acting—showing people how to connect in ways that inspire compassionate results. NVC is now being taught around the globe in communities, schools, prisons, mediation centers, churches, businesses, professional conferences, and more. Hundreds of certified trainers and hundreds more supporters teach NVC to tens of thousands of people each year in more than sixty countries.

CNVC believes that NVC training is a crucial step to continue building a compassionate, peaceful society. Your tax-deductible donation will help CNVC continue to provide training in some of the most impoverished, violent corners of the world. It will also support the development and continuation of organized projects aimed at bringing NVC training to high-need geographic regions and populations.

To make a tax-deductible donation or to learn more about the valuable resources described below, visit the CNVC website at www. CNVC.org:

- **Training and Certification**—Find local, national, and international training opportunities, access trainer certification information, connect to local NVC communities, trainers, and more.

- **CNVC Bookstore**—Find mail or phone order information for a complete selection of NVC books, booklets, audio, and video materials at the CNVC website.

- **CNVC Projects**—Participate in one of the several regional and theme-based projects that provide focus and leadership for teaching NVC in a particular application or geographic region.

For more information, please contact CNVC at:
Ph: 505-244-4041 • US Only: 800-255-7696 • Fax: 505-247-0414
Email: cnvc@CNVC.org • Website: www.CNVC.org

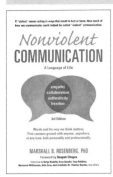

Nonviolent Communication, 3rd Edition
A Language of Life
By Marshall B. Rosenberg, PhD

$19.95 — Trade Paper 6x9, 264pp, ISBN: 978-1-892005-28-1

What Is "Nonviolent" Communication?
It is the integration of 4 things:

Consciousness: a set of principles that support living a life of
compassion, collaboration, courage, and authenticity
Language: understanding how words contribute to connection
or distance
Communication: knowing how to ask for what we want, how to hear others even in
disagreement, and how to move toward solutions that work for all
Means of influence: sharing "power with others" rather than using "power over others"

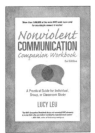

Nonviolent Communication Companion
Workbook, 2nd Edition
A Practical Guide for Individual, Group, or Classroom Study
By Lucy Leu

$21.95 — Trade Paper 7x10, 240pp ISBN: 978-1-892005-29-8

Putting NVC Skills Into Practice!

Learning Nonviolent Communication has often been equated with
learning a whole new language. *The NVC Companion Workbook* helps you put these
powerful, effective skills into practice with chapter-by-chapter study of Marshall Rosenberg's
cornerstone text, *NVC: A Language of Life*. Create a safe, supportive group learning or practice
environment that nurtures the needs of each participant. Find a wealth of activities, exercises,
and facilitator suggestions to refine and practice this powerful communication process.

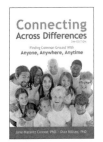

Connecting Across Differences, 2nd Edition
Finding Common Ground With Anyone, Anywhere, Anytime
By Jane Marantz Connor, PhD and Dian Killian, PhD

$19.95 — Trade Paper 6x9, 416pp, ISBN: 978-1-892005-24-3

Connection Is Just a Conversation Away!

This fully revised second edition offers an accessible guide for exploring
the concepts, applications, and transformative power of the Nonviolent
Communication process. Discover simple, yet transformative skills to
create a life of abundance, building the personal, professional, and community connections you
long for. Now with an expanded selection of broadly applicable exercises, role-plays, and activities.
Detailed and comprehensive, this combined book and workbook enhances communication skills
by introducing the basic NVC model, as well as more advanced NVC practices.

**Available from PuddleDancer Press, the Center for Nonviolent Communication, all major
bookstores, and Amazon.com. Distributed by Independent Publisher's Group: 800-888-4741.
For Best Pricing Visit: NonviolentCommunication.com**

The Healing Power of Empathy
True Stories About Transforming Relationships
Edited by Mary Goyer, MS

$17.95 — Trade Paper 6x9, 288pp, ISBN: 978-1-934336-17-5

Empathy Is a Learnable Skill!

Empathy is the cornerstone of good relationships—but it can be hard to access when it's most needed. Luckily, empathy is also a learnable skill, with the power to move conversations out of gridlock and pain.

- See how anger and blame get translated and how productive dialogues are made possible.
- Hear the words used to repair arguments before they cause damage.
- Watch how self-empathy transforms relationships—without speaking any words at all.

Dementia Together
How to Communicate to Connect
By Pati Bielak-Smith

$17.95 — Trade Paper 6x9, 248pp, ISBN: 978-1-934336-18-2

Build a Healthy Dementia Relationship!

If you are looking to build and sustain a healthy relationship with someone who has dementia, this book is for you.

Dementia is an illness that causes no physical pain. Yet ask anyone who cares about someone with Alzheimer's or another dementia if their heart isn't aching. The pain in dementia comes not from the illness, but from feeling hopeless, alone, or disconnected from someone you care about. And a broken relationship can be healed.

Collaborating in the Workplace
A Guide for Building Better Teams
By Ike Lasater
With Julie Stiles

$7.95 — Trade Paper 5-3/8x8-3/8, 88pp, ISBN: 978-1-934336-16-8

Foster Superior Collaboration!

What can individuals do to improve the ability of teams to collaborate and create powerful outcomes? *Collaborating in the Workplace* focuses on the key skills that research shows support effective collaboration and the practical, step-by-step exercises that individuals can practice to improve those skills. By using this book, people can work better together to create outstanding outcomes.

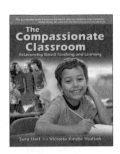

The Compassionate Classroom
Relationship Based Teaching and Learning
By Sura Hart and Victoria Kindle Hodson

$17.95 — Trade Paper 7.5x9.25, 208pp, ISBN: 978-1-892005-06-9

When Compassion Thrives, So Does Learning!

Learn powerful skills to create an emotionally safe learning environment where academic excellence thrives. Build trust, reduce conflict, improve co-operation, and maximize the potential of each student as you create relationship-centered classrooms. This how-to guide offers customizable exercises, activities, charts, and cutouts that make it easy for educators to create lesson plans for a day, a week, or an entire school year. An exceptional resource for educators, homeschool parents, child-care providers, and mentors.

Respectful Parents, Respectful Kids
7 Keys to Turn Family Conflict Into Co-operation
By Sura Hart and Victoria Kindle Hodson

$17.95 — Trade Paper 7.5x9.25, 256pp, ISBN: 978-1-892005-22-9

Stop the Struggle—Find the Co-operation and Mutual Respect You Want!

Do more than simply correct bad behavior—finally unlock your parenting potential. Use this handbook to move beyond typical discipline techniques and begin creating an environment based on mutual respect, emotional safety, and positive, open communication. *Respectful Parents, Respectful Kids* offers *7 Simple Keys* to discover the mutual respect and nurturing relationships you've been looking for.

Peaceful Living
Daily Meditations for Living With Love, Healing, and Compassion
By Mary Mackenzie

$19.95 — Trade Paper 5x7.5, 448pp, ISBN: 978-1-892005-19-9

Live More Authentically and Peacefully!

In this gathering of wisdom, Mary Mackenzie empowers you with an intimate life map that will literally change the course of your life for the better. Each of the 366 meditations includes an inspirational quote and concrete, practical tips for integrating the daily message into your life. The learned behaviors of cynicism, resentment, and getting even are replaced with the skills of Nonviolent Communication, including recognizing one's needs and values and making choices in alignment with them.

Available from PuddleDancer Press, the Center for Nonviolent Communication, all major bookstores, and Amazon.com. Distributed by Independent Publisher's Group: 800-888-4741. For Best Pricing Visit: NonviolentCommunication.com

About the Author

Jim Manske has made a lifelong exploration of the types of practices that make peace not only possible but inevitable. Growing up in the 1960s, he heard everybody around him say they wanted peace, "but everywhere I looked, I saw conflict . . . between friends and family, between neighbors, in civil rights battles and the escalating war in Vietnam—it was us versus them everywhere!" His journey thus began with a sense that the way people speak and listen to one another contributes to either war or peace in each moment. He went on to study and develop skills in communication, psychology, spirituality, personal growth, mediation, facilitation, and peacemaking. Then, in 2000, he attended his first workshop with internationally recognized peacemaker Marshall Rosenberg. "Within fifteen minutes, I knew my life would never be the same."

Jim has now been learning and sharing Nonviolent Communication for more than twenty years. He is a certified trainer and assessor for the Center for Nonviolent Communication and co-creator of the learning tool Pathways to Liberation Self-Assessment Matrix, which has been translated into sixteen languages and is used globally by NVC practitioners working toward trainer certification. He and his partner, Jori, also a CNVC certified trainer, live and work together in Maui. Their goal is to build a global network of friends devoted to practicing peace by fully integrating NVC into their lives and communities.